Proud to be Liberal

*T
Thanks for coming to my concert!*

*DAVID
H-W*

Proud to be Liberal

**Edited by
Elizabeth Clementson and Robert Lasner**

Brooklyn, New York

Ig Publishing
178 Clinton Avenue
Brooklyn, NY 11205

www.igpub.com

Library of Congress Cataloging-in-Publication Data

Proud to be liberal / edited by Elizabeth Clementson and Robert Lasner.
    p. cm.
  ISBN-13: 978-0-9752517-6-8
  ISBN-10: 0-9752517-6-7
  1. Liberalism—United States. 2. Political culture—United States. I.
Clementson,
Elizabeth, 1973- II. Lasner, Robert.
  JC574.2.U6P76 2006
  320.510973—dc22
                        2005034520

"Patriotic Liberals Enlist in the War of Ideas" adapted from WHAT WE
STAND FOR: *A Program for Progressive Patriotism Edited by Mark Green.*
Copyright © 2004 by The New Democracy Project. Reprinted by
permission of Newmarket Press, 18 E. 48th Street, New York, NY 10017,
1-800-669-3903, www.newmarketpress.com.

Contents

Introduction

On October 8, 2004, like millions of Americans we were watching the second presidential debate between President George Bush and the Democratic challenger, John Kerry. Very early in the debate, Bush hit Kerry with the charge that we all knew was coming, as it had been a central pillar of Bush's campaign strategy: that Kerry was a liberal.

After saying, with derision, that the *National Journal* had named Kerry the "most liberal senator," Bush went on to detail how Kerry was going to "tax everybody to fund his programs," and how "[his plan] would ruin the quality of health care in America." Why would those terrible things happen if Kerry were elected? Because, as Bush eagerly pointed out, "That's what liberals do." Bush finished off his attack by saying that Kerry's potentially ruinous ideas "[fit] with his [liberal] philosophy."

We had a good idea of how Kerry would respond to this, and sadly, we weren't disappointed. "The president is just trying to scare everybody here with throwing labels around," Kerry said. "I mean, seriously—labels don't mean anything." Like pretty much every Democrat over the past 20 years, Kerry was running from the "liberal" label.

It was at that moment that the idea for this book came about. We decided that it was time for someone to finally stand up and say what should have been said the first time the word "liberal" came under siege from the right: that liberalism was responsible for many of the things that have made this country great, and that liberalism is what can make this country great again.

After Barry Goldwater's stinging defeat in the 1964 presidential election, the Republican Party reorganized with two interrelated goals in mind: to win elections, and in the process, undo the gains of liberalism that had effectively changed this country over the first half of the 20th century. The "New America" they envisioned was in fact an old one, one in which the liberal policies—Social Security, Medicare, civil rights, etc.—that many Americans now take for granted would be destroyed.

Led by a combination of newly established Republican think tanks such as the Heritage Foundation, as well as outspoken religious groups such as Jerry Falwell's Moral Majority, this "New Right" coalition was comprised chiefly of southern Democrats who had been alienated by LBJ's embrace of civil rights, and groups who had traditionally been apolitical—primarily Christian evangelicals. Their work throughout the 1970s culminated in the election of Ronald Reagan in 1980. While Reagan's election may have been a "morning in America" for the right, it was the beginning of a "mourning in America" for the left.

The right could not have been successful in their demonization of liberalism, however, if it weren't for the acquiescence of the left. Over the past two decades, Democrats have gone out of their way to dissociate themselves from the liberal label. During the 1988 presidential campaign, Michael Dukakis's response to the "liberal question" was tepid and halting. In 1992, Bill Clinton, taking a page from the Republicans, dubbed himself a "new kind of Democrat," who wouldn't be beholden to the liberal policies of the past, as he so clearly stated in the 1996 State of the Union address, when he declared that the era of big government was over. And then there was John Kerry, decorated Vietnam vet, courageous war protestor and, based on his Senate record, a true liberal, doing everything he could to avoid being tagged with the dreaded moniker.

With this fear of the word "liberal" came a concurrent shift to the right inside the Democratic Party. "Look at our platform," Walter Mondale said as far back as 1984, during his acceptance speech for the Democratic Nomination for President. "There are no defense cuts that weaken our security, no business taxes that weaken our economy, no laundry lists that raid our treasury." Not only did the left now speak the language of the right, they had moved their positions to the right as well. The result was the elimination of the liberal viewpoint from our political discourse.

One of the right's most effective strategies in the current age of media has been turning "liberal" into a dirty word, akin to "anti-American," "Communist," even, "Nazi." All a Republican has to do is call someone a liberal to discredit them.

Attacking liberals is not a new thing. In the 60s liberals were referred to as "bleeding-heart's" to describe those who opposed the Vietnam War and favored government assistance for the poor. But at least back then, when attacked, liberals stood up and defended themselves. This type of passion has been sadly lacking over the past few decades.

Even those on the left who still have some fight in them have become bogged down in the label battle, as the current fascination with alt-liberal terms such as "progressive" or "leftist" or "radical" shows. While there is nothing wrong with calling yourself any of these things, those who use such terms to define themselves miss a larger point: to the majority of Americans, the battle is between "liberals" and "conservatives," and calling yourself something else effectively transforms you from participant to sideline observer in the struggle. While it may be a sad commentary on today's political discourse that we have to so simplify things, this is, unfortunately, where things stand. In our media-drenched world, the fight over labels causes disunity among people on the left who agree on most issues, and distracts us from fighting the real enemy. In this case, John Kerry was right—labels don't mean anything.

Although only one out of every five Americans currently identify themselves as liberal, a majority of Americans still support and believe in liberal programs, like Social Security. While Republicans have been popularizing name-calling in thirty-second sound bites, discussions about the issues have been pushed aside. And so, while we're distracted with hate rhetoric, conservatives have been able to advance their goals of rolling back the gains of liberal movement.

The first lesson you learn as a child when confronted by a bully is to stand up to him. Right now, the Donkey is not standing up to Elephant. As long as Democrats and those on the left run from the "L-Word," Republicans will hunt them down with it. Our only choice is to stand up to the right-wing bullies whom we have been allowing to push us around for far too long. Too many on the left have become unaccustomed to fighting; compromise has ruled too many a day and ruined too many of the liberal policies that revolutionized this country. There is a risk to standing up and fighting—you may get knocked down or end up with a bloody nose—but only by standing up and fighting do you have a chance to win.

The participants in this collection have chosen to stand up and fight.

Elizabeth Clementson
Robert Lasner
December 2005

History: When Liberals Walked the Earth

Liberal? Hell Yes I Am!

By Eric Zorn

Eric Zorn is a 1980 graduate of the University of Michigan, where he was a senior editor at the *Michigan Daily* and a creative writing/English literature major. In 1986, he became a news-feature columnist at the *Chicago Tribune*. That column, "Hometowns," gradually evolved into the commentary column that bears his name. He is a co-author of the 1990 book *Murder of Innocence*, an exploration of the life and tragic rampage of Winnetka schoolhouse killer Laurie Dann.

In my home state of Illinois, and probably in your state as well, we see it in the various attack faxes and scorching e-mails with which the political parties fight their public relations battles. When a strongly conservative candidate rises to prominence—the homophobic firebrand Alan Keyes, for instance, who marched into the Land of Lincoln in 2004 to run for the U.S. Senate—the Democrats brand him as an "arch-conservative," "an ultra-conservative," "an extreme conservative," and so on.

But Republican attacks on Democrats nearly always stop with the shuddering, accusatory word "liberal." The term, they feel, has become so ugly to so many that it needs no modifier like "arch" or "ultra" to do its dirty work; as such terms have become implicit with the word "liberal," they are now redundant.

Many Democrats, accordingly, shun the label—disown it as if it were "libertine" or "leper." They prefer "moderate" or "progressive."

"Liberal," though, is a perfectly good word, and liberalism has a legacy to be proud of. Liberalism is not goofy, it is not soft-headed, it is not seditious, ruinous or ignorant of human nature. Liberalism is the philosophy that best addresses the perpetual conflict between human rights and the exercise of human freedom; it is the philosophy that recognizes that concentrations of power and wealth can lead to evil, whether that concentration lies with the state or with the private sector; and that government at its best is a balancing act, protecting the powerless from forces in society that, unchecked, will cause them harm.

Conservatives have for years been beating the drum that "government" and "regulation" and "taxes" and "limits on capitalism" are categorically suspect. But even they recognize that we need government. We may need less of it in some areas, more of it in others and wiser deployments of resources all the way around. But the lesson of history is that unregulated commerce, the Darwinian pursuit of self-interest, self-aggrandizement and profit by individuals and corporations leads not to some magical, moral, prosperous nirvana, but to cruelty and chaos, to exploitation, degradation of the planet, repression, racism, sexism, poverty, starvation and ultimately violence.

I don't mean to suggest that contemporary conservatives wish or intend for such things. I give them that benefit of the doubt, even though they would have you believe—and seem to have far too many people convinced—that liberals would like nothing better than to create a socialist economic state in which free sexual expression is not just tolerated but mandated, and religion is criminalized.

If liberals are sometimes guilty of romanticizing the beneficial possibilities of government, that foolishness is more than matched by the romantic, even superstitious faith that conservatives place in the—quote, unquote—free market.

Liberalism has its philosophical roots in utopianism—the fantasy of the Enlightenment and the French Revolution that the natural order of things is perfection and that government ought to get out of the way as much as possible to let rational human beings exercise their reason and their rights in what will become a more or less perfect world. This thinking resembles what we today would call libertarianism.

Some historians will argue that the Constitution of the

United States is a quintessentially liberal document because of the way that it enshrines the rights of individuals and seeks through separation of powers to check the impulses of government and majority passions. It's hard to say for sure, because liberalism is not a set of rigid ideals or a dogma that one can track unerringly through the ages or apply with confidence to every social and political issue.

It once meant an embrace of free markets; the belief in their ultimate goodness was a classically liberal idea. Adam Smith was considered a liberal for his belief that "by pursuing his own interest, man frequently promotes that of the society more effectually than when he really intends to promote it."

This airy confidence in the coincident growth of freedom, equality and opportunity looked a whole lot better when Smith wrote it and other liberals advanced it than it did in the late-19th and early-20th centuries, when an increasingly industrial society began exposing key elements of this philosophy as incomplete. "Naïve" probably doesn't overstate it.

It turned out that if you leave a factory owner or a railroad builder or a mine operator or the owner of the Standard Oil company to give free exercise to what he considers his natural rights, he does not typically look to Ben and Jerry for advice on workers' rights. He'll exploit his workers, brutalize them, subjugate them and in a very literal sense, kill them: Witness such bloody attempts to quell the labor movement as the Ludlow Massacre in Colorado in 1914, or such consequences of unsafe workplaces as the Triangle Shirtwaist Co. fire in New York in 1911, where 146 workers died, or the Imperial Food Products fire in Hamlet, N.C., in the 1980s in which 25 workers were trapped and died in a chicken-processing warehouse.

The employer is known to cut whatever safety and environmental corners he thinks will help maximize short-term profits; yet, for some reason, Adam Smith's "unseen hand" does not reach out to keep workers and consumers safe and the air and water clean.

As writer John Judis has noted, "By the dawn of the twentieth century, the balance between liberty and equality had been lost as the unhampered growth of free enterprise led to great corporations, urban slums, and a large, unruly, and underpaid immigrant working class increasingly drawn to radical politics." Judis quotes Herbery Croly, the founder and first editor of the *New Republic*: "The traditional American confidence in individual freedom has resulted in a morally and socially undesirable distribution of wealth. Moreover, these 'gross inequalities' threatened the 'social bond' on which democracy was based."

Looking back, what's surprising is that this was at all surprising to anyone. The institution of slavery—pervasive in all but recent history—illustrates pretty well that the human desire for acquisition, power and self-advancement, while not necessarily immoral, was not necessarily moral either.

And since the broad goal of liberalism was to enhance the dignity, autonomy and opportunity of individuals by protecting them from the powerful forces that have a tendency to usurp those rights, liberals found themselves examining the principal economic basis for their philosophy and saying, "never mind."

Contemporary liberalism, which got its start around 1900, realized that the market economy could itself be a tyrant, as cruel and subjugating and hostile to individuals as any bureaucracy, any monarch, any church.

These entities—business, government, religion—seek power and influence and often the wealth that goes with it. We all seek these things to some degree. It's part of our nature, and

I'd be the last to argue that this is necessarily all bad. In many ways it is a good thing, a spur to action, to greatness, to progress, a spur to jobs. Nothing wrong with that kind of striving, with that kind of power. Bill Gates strove to be the king of software and not only employed thousands but made my life and probably yours easier.

But when that power accumulates, there often seems to be enough darkness in human nature to turn things ghastly for those left without.

Too much government is tyranny, fascism, oppression. Too little government tilts us toward anarchy, toward a brutal form of survival of the fittest in which those who can fill the power void will, and those who can be abused and subjugated—historically women, racial and religious minorities, immigrants, children, the elderly, homosexuals, the disabled and laborers—will be. Contemporary liberalism, at its finest, fights against this abuse and subjugation and curbs those instincts of the powerful and, indeed, considers those curbs morally imperative.

Conservatism, on the other hand, fights against the imposition of those curbs, particularly when it comes to business and the church. Conservatism has adopted the faith in the free market that liberalism abandoned, while its partisans have argued for a greater role in public life for religion, all as part of conservatism's passion for order and traditional institutions.

Conservatives even embrace government power in many areas. Their antigovernment slogans notwithstanding, they don't mind government at all when it comes to using the force of law to control what consenting people do and think and read, to invade their privacy, dictate their morals and, when they are suspected of wrongdoing, to brutalize them.

If liberalism is rooted in a utopian view of the inherent goodness of human beings, conservatism, all the way back to at least Edmund Burke in the late eighteenth century, has been rooted in an anti-utopian view of the inherent evil in human beings. The rude masses were not fit to rule themselves or to think for themselves, and under such a construct personal liberties, a free press, jury trials and so on became absurd. The elites and the church could handle such things.

Well, conservatism has changed, too, with the times. Contemporary conservatives, many of whom I believe are well-motivated, would argue that today's pragmatic conservatives have their philosophical hands full fighting against the excesses of the liberal instinct, the needless and counterproductive curbs liberals want to put on certain forms of behavior.

And they are not always wrong. I'll concede some liberal failings, to be sure. But I'd observe that American society today and American people today are overwhelmingly and happily liberal by the standards of history.

In fact it's my contention that if you were to make a list of the statements to which most people who today call themselves conservative would subscribe, then send a self-proclaimed conservative, say Rush Limbaugh, back in time about 140 years or so and force him to proclaim that list from a stage in a public park, the townsfolk would hang him on the spot as a wild-eyed radical:

"Blacks should be allowed to vote. Women should be allowed to vote. The military and schools should be fully integrated. We must have universal public education. Marriage between different races should be legal. Workers should be allowed the right to organize." And so on.

Conservative pundit George Will wrote not long ago that a return to life as it was in 1900 "is a serviceable summation of the conservatives' goal." Will's wish invites a thought experiment: What would life be like today if the identifiably conservative point of view had held sway at every turn since 1900?

I envision a land of enforced conformity, censorship and little personal privacy where women and blacks are treated as subhuman; a land where the unharnessed free market runs roughshod over employees, nearly all of whom work as temps so that short-term profits can be maximized; a land that victimizes consumers. One could walk from Cleveland to Port Stanley on the industrial slime that was once Lake Erie; public school teachers each morning would lead students in prayers to Jesus; the poor would fend for themselves in third-world-style ghettos; the elderly would be on their own for health care; and everything for children, from schools to libraries, would be privatized so that those who have could have more.

It is the liberal impulse, the progressive impulse, that has given us integration in society, that has greatly expanded the rights of women, that has given us Social Security, electricity in rural areas, guaranteed bank deposits, Head Start, the GI Bill, school lunch programs, truth in packaging, and has protected true freedom or worship. It's liberals who seek to safeguard collective bargaining and limit the workplace exploitation of children, liberals who advanced the cause of clean air and water and safe consumer products, liberals who gave us public housing, aid to families with dependent children and the graduated income tax. It was also liberals who led the fight against certain forms of heavy-handed government, who have tried through the ACLU and other organizations to safeguard freedom of speech, privacy rights, and the right to fair treatment by all from the police and the courts. Remember, liberalism gave this country a New Deal because the old deal had turned out to be such a bad one.

George McGovern, in a December 2002 *Harper's* magazine essay, "The Case for Liberalism," wrote that "If we assume that Lincoln, the first Republican president, was liberal—which he surely was—nothing inspiring has come out of the conservative mind since the age of John Adams. . . ."

He continued by saying, "Virtually every step forward in our history has been a liberal initiative taken over conservative opposition. . . . I challenge my conservative friends to name a single federal initiative now generally approved by both of our major parties that was not first put forward by liberal over the opposition of conservatives . . . How could anyone read history and not be a liberal?"

Interestingly, even some well-known conservatives have wide liberal streaks. In an article in the February/March 2003 *Washington Monthly*, Joshua Green noted wryly that the "federal government expanded (during Ronald Reagan's presidency). . . . [T]he conservative desire to outlaw abortion was never seriously pursued. Reagan broke with the hardliners in his administration and compromised with the Soviets on arms control. His assault on entitlements never materialized; instead he saved Social Security in 1983. And he repeatedly ignored the fundamental conservative dogma that taxes should never be raised. . . . [I]n speeches Reagan continued to repeat his bold pledge to 'get government out of the way of the people,' but 'the number of workers on the federal payroll rose by 61,000 under Reagan." (By comparison, under Clinton, the number fell by 373,000.)

Green goes on to say that "by expanding rather than scaling back entitlements, Reagan . . . demonstrated that conservatives could not and would not launch a frontal assault on Social Security, effectively conceding that these cherished New Deal programs were central features of the American polity."

Today's liberals are hardly alone in their belief that government is needed to support and enforce individual rights, to cushion individuals from the ups and downs of an economically and socially hazardous world. But liberals believe that is the definition of a free society, not a definition that says the consequence of freedom is that power, control and money go to whoever can grab them, and government exists primarily to protect people and private property from immediate physical harm. As John F. Kennedy put it in a 1960 campaign speech, liberalism is "an attitude of mind and heart, a faith in man's ability, through the experience of his reason and judgment, to increase for himself and his fellow men the amount of justice and freedom and brotherhood which all human life deserves."

Most conservatives today will say, yeah, well, so liberals were right about race and gender and...the environment . . . and workplace safety . . . and health care for the elderly and poor . . . and rights of workers to organize . . . and . . . well, enough. We've come a long way with them, but we don't need them anymore.

Wrong.

We still need liberals when conservatives concerned about illegal immigration in California move to punish the children of those immigrants, not the employers who feed the problem by cheerfully hiring illegals.

We still need liberals when, in the name of progress, conservatives are cutting funds for enforcement of workplace health and safety laws and for protection of our clean air and water.

We still need liberals when the minimum wage reaches a 40-year low in terms of purchasing power and the conservatives who strive to keep it there continue to gripe and wonder about the unmotivated underclass.

We still need liberals when industry's response to the diminished power of unions is to accelerate downsizing and outsourcing.

We still need liberals when the income gap between rich and poor yawns to its greatest width since such records have been kept, and conservatives simply deny the social significance of this and make excuses for CEOs who earned only 35 times the salary of an average U.S. worker 25 years ago but now, according to recent estimates, make more than 200 times the average salary.

We still need liberals when conservatives want to cut legal aid for the poor and repeal the National School Lunch Act of 1946, the Child Nutrition Act of 1966 and the Emergency Food Assistance Act of 1983.

We still need liberals when America has higher rates of infant mortality, illiteracy, malnutrition and poverty than any other advanced, civilized nation.

We still need liberals when conservatives are willing to torch the ideals of the Constitution in order to take their revenge upon the small handful of idiots who burn the American flag.

And we still need liberals when the criminal justice and legislative systems staunchly refuse to enact meaningful reforms in police, prosecution and court procedures that now routinely send innocent men and women to prison and to Death Row.

Conservatives love to hit me with the old one-liner, "A conservative is a liberal who has just been mugged." The traditional response to this is, ". . . and a liberal is a conservative who's just been arrested." I've added that a liberal is a conservative who has lost his job or his health insurance, found out his child is gay, learned that his 15-year-old daughter is pregnant or heard that his 18-year-old in the military is being sent overseas to fight to protect the American oil industry.

Another favorite conservative adage is "If you're not a liberal at age 20, you have no heart. If you're still a liberal at age 40, you have no head." What's not to love about an adage that suggests that you are both smarter and more mature than those with whom you disagree? There's certainly truth to the observation that outlooks and attitudes change as we get older. And two of the major changes—becoming more risk averse and growing more cynical—are associated with a drift toward conservatism. We become more risk averse as we acquire more responsibilities. It's easier to take chances—to experiment with new ideas, to trust in the good of mankind, to put your money on dreams and visions—when you don't have a mortgage and kids to worry about and champagne tastes to support in your looming retirement years.

We also become more cynical as experience teaches us the grim reality of human nature and the futility of simple, utopian solutions to complex problems. Gradually, we learn that many of our movement leaders, secular saints and supposed altruists are self-aggrandizing hypocrites. We find that programs to lift up, educate or employ the downtrodden are too often run by pocket-stuffing protectors of swollen fiefdoms, and that life's apparent victims are often far from blameless for their circumstances.

As the years go by, events batter the liberal's faith in the inherent goodness of the individual and the ability of government to channel it. So he ends up (in my case, anyway) abandoning such ideas as reforming campaign-finance laws, ending the private ownership of handguns and curing poverty with transfusions of cash.

The increasingly cynical person tests his assumptions more and more often. But cynicism turns liberals into conservatives only when they focus their emerging skepticism narrowly. Many nouveau right-wingers fail to examine with a withering eye their own growing faith in free markets, law enforcement and enforced moral conformity, to name three totems of conservatism. Each totem, not uncoincidentally, promises in theory to create a less risky society for those who have acquired a substantial stake in it.

In my case, any shift you detect is a diminished trust in the nostrums and platitudes of ideologues all along the social and political spectrum. In other words, I'm not becoming a Republican, I'm becoming a crank.

In my late 40s, I see more clearly than ever that a key failing of the liberal approach in the modern world has been blindness to the simple fact that it is not only the politician, the business owner, the church leader, the policeman and others with obvious power who need to be restrained lest they harm others. Liberals have not seen that it is also individuals, ordinary citizens, those commonly defined and thought of as powerless. These people, alone and in groups, also have a tendency to abuse, to take advantage, to exploit when they are able.

Unions can be seen as an example of this—enforcing rules in the name of worker protection that end up not only offending the cherished connection between effort and reward but also harming businesses, and, most notably, the customers, the everyday citizens, who patronize those businesses.

The poor. There are welfare loafers, cheats, rank freeloaders who have been empowered by the welfare system—which was designed to protect them—to the point that they are taking advantage of—"exploiting"—those everyday citizens who help pay their way. It should not be a sin against liberal orthodoxy to declare that such people exist. It also should not be a sin against liberal orthodoxy to condemn such people, to demand honest effort from them, to hold them at least somewhat accountable.

The sexually irresponsible. Liberals reject the idea that government or church influences should control sexual expression among consenting adults. They recognize this as incompatible with human liberty. But to the extent that encouraging sexual license has weakened marriage, liberals have to realize that children—the true powerless innocents in virtually any paradigm—suffer and have suffered. It should not be a sin against liberal orthodoxy to defend and encourage lasting commitments, to warn against sexual exploitation and experimentation that experience has shown us can bring harm and heartache to others.

Criminals. The ultimate petty exploiters of the powerless. But in proclaiming our concern that they not be unfairly used by the justice system, we liberals have yielded the anticrime high ground to the so-called "law and order" crowd, whose solutions to this problem are often expensive, counterproductive and brutal in ways that threaten the innocent as well as the guilty. We have ceded that territory because we have focused too much of our concern on the criminal—how he was warped by a rough upbringing and perhaps abused by the justice system—and not enough concern on the actual victim . . . the innocent who has been harmed. In our concern for rehabilitation, reform and rights, we have failed, due to a misunderstanding of the meaning of liberalism, to stand up for law and order. In our tendency to attack and mistrust institutions, we have failed to be in the forefront of a demand for tough, smart, effective and fair enforcement of just laws.

Bureaucrats. Liberals believe in government's ability to address problems and provide solutions. And it is a belief born out by a litany of successes: The Earned Income Tax Credit. Head Start. FEMA. The Clean Water Act. Centers for Disease

Control. Medicare. Medicaid. The EPA. OSHA. The Consumer Product Safety Commission. The GI Bill. The Interstate Highway System. The National Park System. The Peace Corps. Sesame Street. The Women and Infant Children Special Supplemental Food Program.

These are not unalloyed successes, of course. Even good programs serving the powerless can become bloated and arrogant and ridiculous. And bloated, arrogant ridiculous programs waste money.

This, again, creates a class of powerless victims. But it has been against liberal orthodoxy to speak out against such waste when it is supposedly in the service of a higher good. It has been against liberal orthodoxy to demand efficiency and performance along with good intentions in government.

Our silence has allowed many commentators to suggest to the mainstream public that liberalism has no integrity. And to the extent that we have failed to see beyond our narrow orthodoxy, they have been right. Liberals have failed to see that their insight about the tendency of institutions to attempt to gather as much power as possible and to abuse that power, to take advantage, seems to be a human trait. Institutions only have this trait because they are made up of human beings, some of whom (not all of whom, but enough of whom) are sufficiently amoral that they cannot be trusted.

How this insight has escaped us is beyond me. The evidence for it is everywhere. Though there may be and is great kindness in the world, great wisdom and gentility and altruism, there is not enough of it to justify a utopian philosophy that says that rational human beings freely exercising their reason and their rights will create anything resembling a perfect world. This historical premise of liberalism is wrong. And if liberalism is going to make any sense in this century, it is going to have to adjust again, as it did around the beginning of the last century, to accommodate the truths that have become obvious. It is going to have to broaden, again, its definition of that which threatens the dignity, autonomy and opportunity of the individual.

We must correct the impression that we don't know or don't care about the difference between individual behavior that is right and wrong, between good and bad. We pride ourselves, after all, on being a moderating influence. And if we don't attempt to broaden that influence, we will lose it.

To the extent that conservatism is motivated by the desire to move us in that direction and balance the most errant of our impulses, I respect it. I talk and write to a lot of people in my line of work; many of them are conservatives, and many of them seem to me to be genuinely concerned with how liberal failings and traditional liberal ideas can harm and have harmed society.

I'm not cynical enough to think that all or even most conservatives are ill-motivated. Yet I do think that too many are overly concerned with simply protecting what they have and guarding their opportunities to acquire more. In their self-interest they fear and distrust people who are not like them and contrive intellectually to blame such people for the difficulties they have and the suffering they endure.

They dislike government when it attempts to force business not to discriminate, not to befoul the environment, not to pay the lowest wages they can get away with. They dislike government when it attempts to redistribute power and influence in society by, in effect, taking some from them and giving it to others.

In conclusion, I don't ask for even the good conservatives to love us. I ask for us to love ourselves . . . to reclaim the L-word as we celebrate its heritage, and try to readapt it for the 21st century.

Those Who Hate Liberals Hate America
By Harvey Wasserman

Free Press senior editor and "Superpower of Peace" columnist Harvey Wasserman is also senior advisor to Greenpeace USA and the Nuclear Information & Resource Service. He is author or co-author of six books, including four on nuclear power and renewable energy, and two histories of the United States. His most recent book, co-authored with Bob Fitrakis, is *How The GOP Stole America's 2004 Election & Is Rigging 2008*. He can be found on the Web at http://harveywasserman.com

The guttural screech of the Limbaugh/Robertson right against all things "liberal" is first and foremost an attack on America itself. The United States is not now and never has been a "Christian nation." But it has always been a liberal nation, right from the get-go. And those who hate liberals really hate the free nation that was born in 1776 and that defines the sane American mainstream to this day.

Today's Foxist dittoheads would have hated all of America's founders: Franklin, Washington, Jefferson, Madison, Adams, Paine, even the father of the modern corporate state, Alexander Hamilton. All were liberals, both classic and modern. The documents they wrote—the Declaration of Independence, the Constitution, the Bill of Rights—were the definition of liberal. Rush's "conservative" rightists would have hated them back then. And though they won't admit it, they hate them now.

The Bill of Rights remains arguably the most clear and powerful statement of liberal thought and action ever written. Its basic ideas and ideals are anathema to everything that today's "Christian" right demands. In particular, the core fundamentalist belief being foisted by today's antiliberal right wing is a hatred of tolerance. The old-time Puritans, whose cultish fanaticism defines today's Christian right, believed that to tolerate another point of view was to show weakness. Those willing to allow free expression of any opinion other than the "one true religion" must themselves be weak, and thus unacceptable in the eyes of an angry God.

This is the real root of the ongoing attack on the "liberal media." Their almost total right-wing dominance of the news business is still not enough for fanatic fundamentalists. Any newspaper or TV or radio station that allows *any* dissenting opinion is by definition a liberal media. It doesn't matter that 99 out of 100 commentators are right wing. The presence of that one liberal indicates weakness, and thus defines the entire medium as liberal. There is zero tolerance among the fundamentalist right for disagreement of any kind with the True Word as they see it. This is precisely what led to the hanging of nineteen "witches" in Salem in the 1690s and what defines the right wing today. It is not enough for conservatives to outnumber their liberal critics; to be whole in the eyes of their hateful God, there must be perfect uniformity.

And thus it is no accident that the very first clause of the First Amendment demands a separation of church and state. "Congress shall make no law respecting an establishment of religion," it says, and then it goes on to guarantee freedom to practice whatever religion one may choose, as well as to speak, write and assemble freely, and to petition the government for grievances. In a world run by today's "conservatives," every one of those rights is a liberal abomination in the eyes of an angry God.

The real reason these right-wingers hate America is because it was born of the Enlightenment. Its three most influential thinkers were Ben Franklin, Thomas Paine and Thomas Jefferson, none of whom the Limbaughs or Robertsons would be able to tolerate for a nanosecond. All three believed in "God" in the deist sense, as a benign divine force that had created the universe and then set it in motion to follow the laws of nature and free will. All three of them knew and despised the angry, vindictive Puritan overlord who slaughtered those "witches" at Salem.

Franklin, Paine and Jefferson also made it clear that they were definitely not Christians. Like many of their Revolutionary cohorts, they were not interested in authoritarian religion, Christian or otherwise.

Franklin was colonial America's best-read writer and publisher, in many ways the true father of our country. Born of humble Puritan origins, he was a world-class scientific genius, the Einstein of the era, as well as the leading diplomat and humorist. *Poor Richard's Almanac* was Colonial America's most widely read periodical. Its writer/publisher helped found the postal, public-library and insurance industries. His vita is legend. He was the only man to sign the Big Three: the Declaration of Independence, the Treaty of Paris (which sealed the Revolution's victory) and the Constitution.

He was also the ultimate liberal. He signed the first abolitionist petition to Congress. Supremely tolerant, he loved beautiful women, fine food, the French, personal freedom, diversity, the Enlightenment, and progress. The great miracle of his life, he wrote in his autobiography, was that he never got a venereal disease. He assiduously courted "the ladies" while seducing France into helping young America free itself from the British. He went to church briefly before fleeing back to his study and laboratory. He supported faith in a divine being but opposed sects that believed themselves the one true religion. Today's fundamentalists would have hated this most American of all thinkers and writers.

Likewise Tom Paine. Theodore Roosevelt later called him a "filthy little atheist" but he was none of the three. His *Common Sense* was the spark that set off our Revolution. Tolerant, open-minded and nonsectarian, Paine was as liberal as Franklin. His faith was in the reason of humans and their ability, in a free society, to find the way to an honorable, productive life. Limbaugh would have had him hung.

And then there's Tom Jefferson: brilliant, learned master architect, ultimate phrase turner, Lockean liberal, ardent non-Christian, deist and definer of the separation of church and state. Despite the immutable contradiction that he was in fact a slave owner, nobody stoked the leftist rhetoric of revolution and democracy, equality and progress better than Tom Jefferson. His words are the stuff of history, as are his long, loving affair with the spirited Sally Hemmings, and their five children and innumerable descendents. Jerry Falwell would have condemned him to burn in hell!

But Jefferson spoke for a nation that loved liberal freedom and liberty. The best of his words are the best of our nation's diverse liberal core, which today's conservatives hate.

As they would that shrimpy James Madison, spouting off about human liberties, combing the state constitutions to draft that ultimate liberal screed, the Bill of Rights. If there's one document that most clearly contradicts the core beliefs of today's conservatism, it's James Madison's Ten Commandments of civil rights and liberty.

Even George Washington, the ultimate war hero (and our leading brewer and hemp grower) stood his ground for liberalism. When offered the kingship of the new America, he refused, saying that the U.S. should remain a republic. Can you imagine George Bush, who never saw battle, doing the same?

The master of Mount Vernon also took pains to make sure his slaves were freed and well cared for upon his death. What a bleeding heart!

As for Hamilton, the darling of the early corporations was a foreign-born bastard. *The National Review* would have liked his monarchism. He set the foundation for the modern American industrial state, from which Murdoch still profits.

But Hamilton indulged in a Clintonesque extramarital affair. And—can you believe it—he spoke in opposition to slavery!

Even John Adams, staunch federalist, distruster of the people, supported the Bill of Rights. When Haitian slaves staged the world's second anti-imperial revolution, Adams made national headlines by having dinner with their envoy, a man of color! Meanwhile his uppity wife Abigail penned one of America's first clear statements demanding women's rights. Limbaugh would have branded her a feminazi!

There are other American icons whom today's right must hate: Abe Lincoln, that ACLU-type lawyer, signing the Emancipation Proclamation, facing down the southerners, displaying what Carl Sandberg called a hint of "lavender"; U.S. Grant, who established Yellowstone Park; Teddy Roosevelt, who advocated conservationism; even Richard Nixon, who signed the Environmental Protection Act. Wimps! Greenies! Bleeding hearts! Eco-terrorists!

Add in centuries of immigration and diversity, and the grassroots beliefs in democracy and toleration that have defined this nation, and you have a United States created in the image of pointy-headed liberal genius. The Declaration of Independence, Bill of Rights, Emancipation Proclamation, national parks and much much more remain the liberal bulwark of world freedom. At the grassroots, among the farmers and workers, sailors and homemakers, America is a nation of nations, and one that has always believed in letting people live their lives and speak their minds.

It is precisely this that the liberal-haters want to destroy. The tolerance. The diversity. The open belief that all people really are created equal, no matter what they may believe or look like or where they came from or which church—if any—they attend. It's for good reason, literally and figuratively, that the word "Christian" does not appear in the Constitution. America has never wanted a bunch of self-appointed bigots telling everyone else what to believe.

That makes the United States a liberal nation, folks. Always has been. "Conservative America" is an oxymoron.

People Have to Have More to Live For Than to Die For

By Blanche Wiesen Cook

Blanche Wiesen Cook is Distinguished Professor of History at John Jay College and the Graduate Center, City University of New York. She is senior editor of the Garland Library of War and Peace, author of *Eleanor Roosevelt: Volume One: 1884-1933*, *Eleanor Roosevelt: Volume 2: The Defining Years, 1933-1938*, *Crystal Eastman on Women and Revolution* and *The Declassified Eisenhower*, and is a former vice-president for research at the American Historical Association.

Progressive liberals are mostly amazed that the word "liberal," which we once perceived at the "vital center," has become the new word for un-American. After all, liberalism was once the alternative to communism, socialism, fascism and, for most of the 20th century, the very definition of Americanism. In 1940, Franklin Delano Roosevelt confronted a country, divided sectionally and politically, much as it is today, and declared: "We will have a liberal democracy, or we will return to the Dark Ages."

The issues then involved race, class and justice. FDR's solution was a New Deal for all Americans, which included public education, public health, publicly supported programs in the arts and sciences, environmental protection, and the creation of new opportunities and job security for all. All of this, of course, involved taxation. New Dealers were influenced by their 19th-century mentor, Justice Oliver Wendell Holmes, who said: "I do not mind paying taxes. With my taxes, I buy civilization!" By 1913 Progressives, Democrats and Republicans alike, agreed: A graduated income tax would democratize, liberalize and improve America. A social contract in an age of war seemed an important way to establish an enlightened citizenry, decent housing and to put an end to industrial slavery and the greedy antics of the "malefactors" of corrupted wealth.

If we pause to consider what the putschites seek today, their goal is to return to the 19th century, before Jane Addams, Lillian Wald, Florence Kelley and Theodore Roosevelt campaigned for expanded opportunities for poor people, playgrounds, public parks, the sanctity of national forests. Bottom line: This is a war against the entire public sector. This war is camouflaged by lies and sweet rhetoric: Leave no child behind means defund public schools and fill our jails to overflowing with adolescent youngsters. We have created the testing-punishment society. For children, it is among the meanest and cruelest in the world.

It is important to note that during the Cold War, the U.S. was in competition with the Soviet Union, and we needed to prove that we excelled in "guns and butter" issues. Hence, our public schools, music and arts programs flourished. There were Pell grants for poor people to attend college and university, and for prison education. Now there is bipartisan silence about poor people. And, let's be clear: Right-wing DLC Democrats share responsibility for this degrading situation. With public programs for the poor ended, the suffering among us have only churches for sanctuary. Now, we are told federal funds may flow again—but only for "faith-based" initiatives.

Liberals to arms! We need to regroup, reconsider, reorganize. For 30 years I have been privileged to study America's great liberals, Dwight David Eisenhower and Eleanor Roosevelt particularly. They have much to tell us about where we might go from here, and how once again to get there. Theirs was a bipartisan liberal tradition. Compared to the putschites, even Ayn Rand libertarians appear progressive. (Remember, they called for "free minds and free markets.") Mind control, the domination of church over state, homelessness, torture, preemptive war, the end of due process and all international law—from the Geneva Accords to the UN treaties—are un-American grotesqueries. They demand an endless rebellion of mind and heart and spirit. We must meet and confer, fight every day boldly and with passion to restore the spirit and essence of our nation.

To see how far along this dastardly path we have crawled, it is important to remember that Dwight David Eisenhower called himself "a militant liberal." On November 16, 1953, he wrote to John Foster Dulles that his administration was "committed to . . . policies that will bring the greatest good to the greatest number. This means that there must be lifted from the minds of men the fears of disaster, poverty, and old age." He campaigned for national health care and appointed former Women's Army Corps commander Oveta Culp Hobby to head his new Department of Health, Education and Welfare. Together with Eleanor Roosevelt and her friend Esther Lape they fought for the kind of single-payer health plan that we still have yet to achieve. Eisenhower pursued other liberal policies: He increased the minimum wage, extended the excess-profits tax and expanded the public-housing program (there was no homelessness under Ike).

Eisenhower also warned the nation of the dangers of the military-industrial complex, which he originally called the congressional-industrial-military complex. And, without realizing it, he also warned us about the current Republican Party. This is what he wrote to his brother Edgar on May 2, 1956: "Should any political party attempt to abolish social security, unemployment insurance, and eliminate labor laws and farm programs, you would not hear of that party again. . . . There is a tiny splinter group, of course, that believes you can do these things. Among them are H.L. Hunt . . . a few other Texas oil millionaires, and an occasional politician or businessman from other areas. Their number is negligible and they are stupid."

Republicans talk about our "ownership society." People like it when they "own" their own cars, and houses, and insurance policies. That there are seven to 10 million homeless Americans, some of whom go to work and to school from their cars and their vans, apparently does not diminish our "ownership" society—and nobody insists on a revitalized federal housing program, brutally defunded by Ronald Reagan. Since the 1980s, not one federal dollar has gone into new housing starts.

Eleanor Roosevelt's work for affordable housing was central to her democratic vision. She always said that governments exist for only one purpose: to make life better for all people. But, she continued, you can never depend on politicians to do anything about that. You have to go door to door, block by block, village by village to get your wants and your needs met. During the 1920s, ER and her friends went "trooping for democracy" to ask potential voters what they wanted, what they needed. She never told people what to think, or how to vote. She asked questions and worked to build movements—movements for women, peace, community.

Despite being a nation of neighbors, we are a very divided country: not red state vs. blue state, but block by block, door to door. The cultural emphasis and vicious slanders against Godless, leftist, queer and elitist secularists (which sounded so familiar to those of us who remember Joe McCarthy's "phony egg-sucking liberal queer and commie" rhetoric) is camouflage. Our mandatory sentencing rules and perverse criminal justice penalties promote a new era of slavery in every state of our embattled union. There is little work in the Mississippi Delta or throughout the rust belt, but there is work in Parchman Prison and every state and federal lock-up.

And then there is this war. Eisenhower said in 1956: "We cannot save Budapest by bombing it." Today we bomb and bomb to bring democracy to an old and proud historical realm. In this place called Iraq—the fertile crescent between the Tigris and Euphrates Rivers—we have failed to read between the pipelines. For those of us who were taught that "History Begins in Sumer," and "Ur is that first site of beginning, the birthplace of Abraham, just east of which is Eden—Basra, Nasariya, the Marshlands," it is strange indeed to contemplate this war for democracy; or the U.S., once a nation defined by the Enlightenment, marching backward into the 4000-year-old war of the book.

After a lifetime of activism, going door to door throughout America and around the world, ER addressed the future. In the last chapter of her final book, *Tomorrow Is Now*, published posthumously in l963, ER called for ardent courage and refortified liberalism:

"Long ago, there was a noble word, LIBERAL, which derived from the word FREE. [libre] Now a strange thing happened to that word. A man named Hitler made it a term of abuse, a matter of suspicion, because those who were not with him were against him, and liberals had no use for Hitler. And then another man named McCarthy cast the same opprobrium on the word. Indeed, there was a time—a short but dismaying time—when many Americans began to distrust the word which derived from FREE . . . One thing we must all do. We must cherish and honor the word FREE or it will cease to apply to us . . ."

To restore that word, some specific questions must immediately be addressed: Who votes, and who counts? Who controls the voting procedures? How do we prepare an educated creative concerned citizenry? There has been a long war against learning in this country. Who will stand up and demand the return to an excellent public education system that honors and nurtures our best gifts? Every other industrialized nation insures health care for its people. Today, U.S. health costs are the highest on the planet; we have health and healing for profit only. Moreover, over 45 percent of the electorate did not vote in the last election.

We have a smaller voter turnout than any other democracy. Why not fine folks who refuse to vote, or reward folks who do vote?

As we confront our future, it is clear that the Cold War ended without a strategy for peace or global betterment. Initially, George Herbert Walker Bush decided that at cold war's end the U.S. might stand finally for the Universal Declaration of Human Rights. With no fanfare, almost in a whisper, his administration persuaded the Senate in 1992 to ratify the civil and political covenant of the Declaration of Human Rights, which Eleanor Roosevelt did so much to achieve.

But it is the United Nations and the promise of a New Deal for the world that have most specifically faced the wrecker in recent administrations. Ronald Reagan stopped paying U.N. dues, and the U.S. declared virtual war on the international body created after World War II with such high hopes for a future of peace and dignity for all people. In 1945, after 50 million dead, the world agreed that a permanent body to debate and consider was better than a planet embroiled in continual warfare. In 2001 George War Bush transformed 9/11 from a crime against humanity to a war against humanity within 24 hours. Already trillions of dollars in debt, his team promises to continue this war beyond the lifetime of everybody living, whatever that means. Engulfed by horror, terror and war, the future hangs on an alternative thread of recognition: People have to have more to live for than to die for. There will be no peace until we reassert the value of life beyond the womb: health, education, opportunity, justice and dignity for all. People of values understand that war is legalized murder. Massacres do not promote democracy, or international security. The challenge before us is the greatest challenge in U.S. history. We must fight for liberal democracy—the rule of law, international law and the promise of human rights.

Proud to Be the Son of Liberals

By Danny Goldberg

Danny Goldberg is CEO of Air America Radio and the author of the book *How the Left Lost Teen Spirit*, as well as co-editor of the anthology *It's a Free Country*.

My role models for defining liberalism are my parents, who adored Franklin Delano Roosevelt, didn't like communism (but were revolted by the excesses of domestic anti-communism), and felt betrayed when Truman distanced himself from labor unions and cozied up to McCarthyism. They supported the civil rights movement, including programs such as affirmative action, believed unreservedly in civil liberties, opposed any kind of violent protest, and were not pacifists but felt there was nothing unpatriotic about questioning the government's foreign policy.

At the Democratic convention of 1936, Franklin Roosevelt expressed the cosmic essence of economic liberalism.

"Governments can err, presidents do make mistakes, but the immortal Dante tells us that Divine Justice weighs the sins of the cold blooded and the sins of the warm hearted on different scales. Better the occasional fault of a government in the spirit of charity than the consistent omission of a government in the ice of its own indifference."

Liberalism represents the most optimistic and idealistic vision of human society as it exists in the United States, the idea that a society can create great wealth but still provide opportunity and decent living conditions for all of its citizens.

There is a large American consensus for the principals behind many liberal ideas, but there is a failure in the political and media culture to connect these principals with programs that live up to them.

Liberalism means public schools. A pure free-market economy

would support only private schools. Once one accepts the idea that society, through its government, has a moral obligation (and a healthy self-interest) in providing education for all of its children, true liberalism requires that the schools be, as much as possible, equally funded. By what logic should schools in poor neighborhoods have worse facilities than those in rich communities?

Liberalism means that there is a minimum wage. A pure market economy would allow wages to fall as low as the most desperate person would be willing to accept. Since it has been demonstrated that the United States has been able to continue to be the world's wealthiest country despite having a minimum wage, what is the moral, political or economic argument that supports keeping it so low? True liberalism requires the minimum wage to keep pace with inflation, the growth of upper-income salaries, the gross national product, etc.

Liberalism means that unions should be free to organize. Anyone who thinks that Orwellian language is a new conservative development need only contemplate "right to work" laws, which exist to allow corporations to make it difficult or impossible for unions to organize. Workers in "right to work" states make much less for comparable work in other states. Stronger unions provide an appropriate balance to the vast power of large corporations.

Liberalism means that society should pay for certain minimum standards of civilization such as electricity and roads in rural areas. True liberalism would add universal health care to that list, at least on a par with other Western countries.

Liberals understand that some tax money is wasted and would always support actions to eliminate waste fraud and abuse. But they would rather pay more taxes in order to live in a society with vibrant public libraries, museums and parks than one with lower taxes in which only the wealthy could participate in civic institutions that are commonplace in other civilized countries.

Liberalism acknowledges that we should enact laws to regulate aspects of businesses that otherwise would damage society, such as pollution or unsafe workplaces.

Liberalism means we have some shared obligation to each other—not only to members of our family or neighborhood or religion or race or political philosophy—but to all of our fellow citizens . . . and that they have that same level of obligation to us.

Not every economic liberal is also a civil libertarian, but I would suggest that "movement liberals" have to also be civil libertarians. Respect for humanity requires the according of individual rights. The "bold persistent experimentation" urged by Roosevelt needs to be given to programs that accord freedom of speech, freedom of religion and the widest practical definition of due process in dealing with the law-enforcement system. There is something inherently illiberal about having as many people in prison as modern America does.

The reason why the word "liberal" became vulnerable while the word "conservative" flourished is that there were some summer soldiers who, while basking in the power of the post-Roosevelt liberal majority, wanted to wrap the word around moderate and conservative political agendas once the political price of true liberalism became uncomfortable for them.

In 1965, when I was in 11th grade, I attended a march on Washington against the Vietnam War at which Carl Ogelsby of the antiwar group Students for a Democratic Society (SDS) railed against the self-described liberals of the Johnson administration who were pursuing the war in Vietnam and who, he said, "broke my liberal heart." Lyndon Johnson was the greatest liberal president since FDR in terms of domestic policy, but his obsession with expanding the war in Vietnam alienated most American liberals.

The alienation was exacerbated by Hubert Humphrey, who had been correctly perceived as a liberal U.S. senator and who, as Johnson's vice-president, refused to criticize the war that most true liberals (and eventually most Americans) felt did America far more harm than good.

Later in the 1960s, there were some Democrats who continued to call themselves liberals (and who had supported the Civil Rights bill) yet opposed affirmative action.

As a result of all this, the word "liberal" became muddied to much of the American left, and when people like Ronald Reagan and later Rush Limbaugh attacked liberalism from the right, many liberals were tepid or silent in their defense of a word that had become so confused in its definition.

For a brief period the word "radical" became shorthand for liberals who were against the war in Vietnam and in favor of programs like affirmative action. But "radical" was ruined by destructive factions that believed in violence, and so it was replaced by "progressive." I have nothing against the word "progressive," but I'm excited about reclaiming the word "liberal" because it connects modern progressive activity with long historical traditions.

Phil Ochs, the great singer-songwriter of the 1960s, wrote a sarcastic song called "Love Me, I'm a Liberal," which made fun of phony liberals. When I played it for my mother she was hurt. She felt it meant that people like her and my dad were hypocrites. But that's not what I meant in my enthusiasm for it. Ochs was identifying those who betrayed the liberal movement, many of whom would reinvent themselves years later as "neoconservatives." My parents and people like them were the true liberals, the ones who make me proud of the word and the politics associated with it.

Why We're Not "Right"

Cure Your Mean Heart, Kill Your Greed: How Liberals Might Save the World from Ruin by Asserting the Primacy of Love Over Hate

By Steve Almond

Steve Almond is the author of the short-story collections *My Life in Heavy Metal* and The *Evil B.B. Chow and Other Stories*, as well as *Candyfreak: A Journey through the Chocolate Underbelly of America*. He teaches creative writing at Boston College.

Many years ago, my grandmother Annie Rosenthal took a job teaching sixth-graders at PS 113 in Harlem. She was a popular teacher and eventually received a promotion to acting assistant principal. She also happened to believe that a culture based on unlimited personal acquisition was morally wrong and that the world's resources should be dispersed according to people's needs, which is to say, in the snarling parlance of the times, she was a "card-carrying member of the Communist party," a crime for which she was eventually forced to resign her post.

So when a glamorous sociopath like Anne Coulter rises from the feculent swamp of Fox News punditry and starts soft-pedaling McCarthyism, the appropriate response is to roll up a copy of the Constitution and jam it down her throat.

Which is to say, this is not going to be the sort of essay that attempts to take a measured look at the political ills of our age and seeks *a healing solution*. The time for healing is long since past. We are living in an era of mind-boggling cruelty, selfishness and selective amnesia.

And we are in this state precisely because the best impulses of this country, the most generous and tolerant impulses—the *adult* impulses—have been overrun by a pack of mean children; they are commonly known as conservatives.

The only way to reverse course is to reassert the moral superiority of liberalism over conservatism, which will require (yes, I'm sorry to be the bearer of bad news) a set of *cajones*.

Though actually, that's not quite right. There's no need to

make assertions. The relative records of conservatism and liberalism are clear. They are not a matter of debate. It is only that the political leadership of the left—and I use the word "leadership" reluctantly—has failed to articulate this record.

Let me offer a few examples.

Fiscal Responsibility

Liberals: After inheriting deficits, Bill Clinton established the largest surplus in the history of the country.

Conservatives: George W. Bush squandered this surplus and, in four years, ran up the largest federal deficit in history. He did so by insisting on massive tax cuts for the rich, while launching two costly wars.

Military Interventions

Liberals: FDR exhorted Americans to join the fight against fascism. Was opposed by conservatives who branded him a warmonger. Only allowed to declare war after the Japanese bombed Pearl Harbor.

Conservatives: Bush went to war against Iraq based on a series of spurious claims, chiefly that Saddam Hussein possessed weapons of mass destruction.

Terrorism

Liberals: Clinton's transition team warned Bush administration that terrorism should be their number-one priority.

Conservatives: Bush took monthlong vacation right before the deadliest terrorist attack ever on American soil. Ignored a memo warning of the imminent attack.

Social Programs
Liberals: Responsible for the New Deal, the Great Society, the War on Poverty.

Conservatives: Have sought to brand social programs as "government handouts." Favor welfare for corporations.

Scandal
Liberals: Clinton was nearly impeached for receiving blowjobs.

Conservatives: Reagan's cabinet was involved in running guns to the death squads in Nicaragua.

The Environment
Liberals: Concerned, based on overwhelming scientific evidence, that the Earth may soon become uninhabitable. Eager to find alternative energy sources.

Conservatives: Favor deregulation and allowing industry lobbyists to write legislation. Believe global warming is a myth. Fully support oil companies.

Religion
Liberals: Believe in the separation of church and state.

Conservatives: Believe prayer in school is essential.

Race Relations
Liberals: Forced the passage of Civil Rights Act.

Conservatives: Fought the Civil Rights movement tooth and nail. In more candid moments, continue to express veiled support for racial segregation (see Lott, Trent).

You will notice a certain inexorable pattern developing here. Conservatives, in short, have a hole where their hearts are supposed to be. Though again, that's not quite right. It's not a hole. It's more like an ulcer, a big, fist-shaped ulcer that keeps pumping bile into their bloodstreams.

Because the conservative record is such an abject failure, and so offensive to basic standards of decency and fairness, right-wingers spend very little time talking about the issues cited above. Instead, they depend on emotional manipulation.

And if you listen to the conservative pundits who beset our media outlets (as I do in moments of uncontrolled masochism), the engine of the ideology quickly becomes clear: hate. Plain and simple hate. Coulter. Limbaugh. Michael Savage. They are all walking hate crimes, hollow fascists. They attack because they have nothing—no basic moral position—to defend.

And who do they attack? Well, it's no longer tenable to publicly revile people of color, so they've found a more acceptable target: liberals.

The conservative agenda has broad ambitions. In economic terms, they favor a smaller government, one that emphasizes self-reliance. It's become conservative dogma to criticize virtually any social program—welfare, Head Start, NEA grants, Medicare—as if they were some giant Communist plot to subvert the will of our poor, beleaguered CEOs.

But the great liberal politicians didn't devise these programs to undermine capitalism, or to mollycoddle those lazy welfare moms Ronald Reagan was so fond of invoking. No, they devised these programs because capitalism was undermining our essential moral duties to one another, as fellow human beings. The rich were getting too rich and the poor were getting too poor. The private interests of a few were replacing the collective interests of the many. Greed was being given precedence over generosity.

John Steinbeck probably expressed this most eloquently in his 1939 novel, *The Grapes of Wrath*, which chronicled the journey of Dust Bowl migrant farmers to California. As they head west, the preacher Jim Casy is told about a man in California who owns a million-acre farm.

"Million acres?" he says. "What in the world can he do with a million acres?"

Naturally, conservatives accused Steinbeck of being red for having the temerity to question the necessity of such concentrated wealth. But the question stands. And it's one that the liberals of this country should have been posing when George W. Bush was rolling back taxes on the richest one percent of the country and gutting the estate tax.

Because the central effect of these policies is fundamentally regressive: We are dragged backward to an era in which the preservation of the aristocracy was the central governing impulse. Not a democracy, in other words, but an oligarchy.

The very idea of liberalism, though, argues that the government should serve as a force for good in the lives of working Americans, not a guardian of the powerful.

The problem is we don't have any real liberals in Washington. We have people like Al Gore and John Kerry, who lack the courage to speak in plain terms about the dangers of greed and bigotry and fear mongering.

To cite a recent example: Bush's desperate effort to "save Social Security" by establishing private accounts. He did this by—surprise, surprise—trying to scare people. He claimed the system was in crisis. According to most experts, it is not. And even if it were, why should the American people trust Bush to solve the crisis? Given his fiscal record, that would be like asking a demolition crew to repair your toilet.

Bush's plan was merely an effort to stimulate a short-term boom in the economy by funneling the rainy-day money of senior citizens into the glittering casinos of Wall Street. The serious economists all understood this. But you didn't have to be an expert to understand the folly of Bush's plan. You need only examine history. The Social Security fund was created to prevent elderly people from starving in the wake of an economic collapse like the one that took place in 1929. The Great Crash, it was called.

Guess what crashed?

Many years ago, a true liberal named Franklin Delano Roosevelt declared: "We have nothing to fear, but fear itself." The conservative movement has made a gruesome truth of this aphorism. In addition to stoking people's hatred, they have ruthlessly exploited people's sense of fear. There is always someone or something we should fear. Initially, it was the Communists. Then the hippies. Then it was crime (which is a code word for the underclass). And now we have the terrorists.

With the attacks of 9/11, the conservatives received the gift of a lifetime. Bush, whose administration had been utterly adrift, was suddenly endowed with the dignity of a steadfast leader. We all got to watch that draft-dodging former frat boy climb onto that pile of rubble and talk tough into a megaphone.

And he wasn't just talking tough—he had a whole army at his disposal. So he went to war with Afghanistan and toppled the Taliban. He created an entirely new bureaucracy, the eerily named Department of Homeland Security, whose chief function has been to keep the populace in a state of perpetual fear. Then he and his minions staged their coup de grace: launching war on Iraq.

It was a truly remarkable achievement. They told two huge lies, over and over again: that Iraq was involved in 9/11, and that Iraq posed a direct threat to the United States. The evidence presented was eventually proved false. If a liberal president had tried to goose step us into a discretionary war using such bogus claims, he would have been impeached faster than you can say Watergate.

But the leadership of the left did nothing more than shrug and sigh. After all, the conservatives had declared a jihad on anyone who didn't support the war. Such heretics were branded traitors. And besides, Saddam fit the part. He was a figure of evil large enough to accommodate the American need to play hero.

And so we went to war and stomped another fifth-rate army and killed a lot of innocent women and children and suffered the loss of thousands of young American soldiers. And where was the vaunted liberal media of which we hear so much talk during the march to war? They were actually doing the administration's bidding. Judith Miller of the *New York Times*, to cite a particularly shameful example, was broadcasting the blatant, pro-war lies of an Iraqi expat named Mohammad Chalabi.

Now, almost three years later, we have killed untold numbers of innocent Iraqis, as well as over 2,000 American soldiers, and are mired in a conflict that has revealed itself as an insane act of hubris, an imperial boondoggle.

A true liberal, though, would have had the courage to stand up and oppose the war from the beginning. A true liberal would have decried the infantile extremism borne of 9/11. A true liberal would have asked that we honor the dead not by creating more corpses, but by demanding a greater humanity of ourselves.

It was perhaps the saddest tableau of the 2004 election to see the Democrats convert their national convention into a lame little war rally, as John Kerry hoped to cash in on his status as a Vietnam hero. The former Swift Boat captain took Boston by sea. He stood on stage with his fellow vets. This feeble attempt to lionize Kerry's service played directly into the conservative plan. Suddenly, Vietnam was being replayed. Only this time, rather than a national disgrace, it was a source of pride.

Kerry the liberal had lost his bearings. The one noble thing he had done, after all, was to protest the war after he came back from combat, to deliver the bad news, to choose honest regret over false pride.

Given the chance to expose his opponent—who had dodged combat, while supporting the war, who was sending young men and women to die in Iraq based on blatant and sustained misrepresentations—Kerry merely stood there and saluted.

If you listen to the conservative demagogues long enough, an eerie thing happens. You start to realize that they are constantly—and I mean constantly—projecting. Every criticism they aim elsewhere is one that they know to be true of themselves.

Liberals are unpatriotic. Liberals are extremists. Liberals don't care about average Americans. My favorite is *Liberals are out of touch with reality.* Oddly, you never hear them speak much about this reality. Because to do so would reveal the depth of their ongoing delusion.

Here, then, is the reality of where we stand in 2006:

- By all assessments (including the administration's) we have reached "peak oil production." In the coming decades, oil will become more and more scarce, and dramatically more expensive to extract or purchase. This will be an abject disaster for the American economy, which is predicated on cheap oil. Even more so, given that the Chinese—a nation of 1.3 billion—will soon be competing for the remaining reserves.

- Our government is trillions of dollars in debt. Much of this debt has been purchased (in the form of treasury bonds) by China and Japan. These nations continue to buy our debt because they need Americans to buy their goods.
- The global economy has placed American workers in direct competition with workers in the developing world, who are willing to do the same work for a fraction of the cost.
- Virtually the entire scientific community agrees that global warming has begun, and many predict that rising sea levels will flood coastlines and turn much of America's arable land into desert.

That, folks, is reality.

And how have the conservatives reacted?

They have ignored every single one of these looming crises, pretended they don't exist, and accused anyone who speaks about them of doom seeking and sedition.

They have had an able leader in this campaign. President Bush has blithely run up the national debt on behalf of his wealthiest constituents. A former oil man himself, he has refused to address our dependence on fossil fuel—he considers global warming a myth. With his encouragement, we continue buying SUVs and building far-flung gated communities and dreaming of becoming rich enough to appear on TV. The Great American Ponzi Scheme grinds on.

A great many citizens (including our president) have found comfort in God, who, they believe, will clean up the mess we make of Earth during the rapture and reserve a place for them in heaven. For those of us not blessed with such faith, the question remains: Are we going to face reality or not?

And here we have reached the essential fallacy of conservatism. They are always talking about how tough they are. But they don't even have the courage to face the reality of our historical circumstance. They have instead retreated into a stance of angry denial, one in which they can regard their moral and material profligacy as a God-given right. Their only discernable creed is social Darwinism: Everyone should get what they can and not worry about the next guy and never be ashamed of their worst impulses. Why? Because America is a great, shining example to the world and we will live forever in freedom and plenty and anyone who tells you otherwise is the enemy.

It is a profoundly naïve stance, the worldview of a frightened, destructive child.

And so the time has come for the adults—those who are mature enough to recognize the perils we face—to intervene.

This is going to require more than love and hope and good intentions. It is going to require rage and activism and perhaps some danger. No entrenched oligarchy cedes its power without a struggle. Which is precisely why I have focused more on the sins of conservatism than the merits of liberalism.

That said, we do live in a democracy, perhaps the most perfect democracy humankind has yet devised. We remain the richest and freest country on earth, and the one most likely to effect positive change in other nations. (By which—to be clear—I do not mean exporting democracy at gunpoint.)

The first step is for the left to reconnect to its righteousness, its radical humanism. And to demand that our leaders reconnect to the core principles of liberalism:

- Government should be a force for good in the lives of the disenfranchised.
- Tolerance, generosity and sacrifice must be our central cultural values.
- The public sector must not be allowed to do the bidding of the private sector.

Liberals must chart a new path based on these tenets. This will involve getting the money and lobbyists out of politics, curing Americans of their oil addiction, seeking alternative fuel sources, addressing the causes of global warming, and a host of other measures. It will involve, in other words, accepting a greater sense of collectivism. The conservative solution is to build barricades and buy guns. But this is a suicidal course; it is only a matter of time before the oil starts to run out, and the oceans rise and the food shortages begin, and by then it will be too late to stave off the violence of panic.

We will either survive as a global collective, or perish in our bunkers.

I realize that the purpose of this volume is to celebrate liberalism. I fully intended to do so, to tell the story of my grandparents and my parents, who all fought for liberal causes, against violence and greed, for a greater compassion between men. But the truth is, they lost. The ideals of liberalism didn't die within them but were beaten down by the forces of fear and hate, by the simple failings of imagination.

I won't be proud to be a liberal, in other words, until the word means something again, until its adherents stand up to the psychopathic bullies in charge of this zoo and reassert the majesty of their beliefs.

Who knows? It might be that the citizens of this country are ready to take a greater responsibility for one another, to choose human connection over withdrawal, to sacrifice on behalf of a shared destiny.

We won't know until we offer them a chance to grow up.

No Apologies, No Regrets

by Ted Rall

Ted Rall is a syndicated cartoonist, columnist, talk show host and occasional war correspondent. Among his many books are *Wake Up You're Liberal: How We Can Take America Back from the Right*.

Being a liberal didn't become something to be proud of until they tried to turn it into a dirty word. For the first four-fifths of the last century, adhering to the core set of values that defines liberals was cause neither for puffery nor shame; it merely made sense. Our nation, dedicated to the pursuit of progress in all things, naturally empathized with those who worked for better standards of living and reduced discrimination over the conservatives who fought tooth and nail to continue the oppressive Bad Old Days. To be sure, lefties transformed the United States from a laissez-faire hellhole of sociopathic selfishness into a society with a sense of joint purpose and responsible empathy. But they were prouder of what they had achieved as Americans than as conquering political partisans.

Ronald Reagan won the presidency in 1980 partly by asserting that liberals were out of ideas. It would have been more precise (if less politic) to say that liberals were victims of their own success. So many of their ideas had been incorporated into mainstream assumptions—that workers were entitled to a living wage, that women and racial minorities deserved the same shot at the American Dream as white males, that giving the down and out a helping hand was in everyone's interest—that they were exhausted from their victorious battles.

Reagan put liberals on the defensive, first by questioning their motives and then by unraveling their hard-fought gains. Liberalism, an aggressive and dynamic ideology devoted to the prospect that we could do better, was thus reduced to playing defense. The same self-doubt that had honed their earlier big ideas led many to wonder aloud whether they'd overreached. Unfortunately, liberal humility was no match for conservative arrogance. And it was a prescription for electoral failure in our "what have you done for me lately" culture.

If liberalism lost its sense of purpose under Reagan-Bush I, however, it lost its meaning under Bill Clinton. Here, after all, was a Democrat who won two elections by distancing himself from liberals and whose major legislative achievements —the NAFTA and GATT "free trade" agreements, welfare "reform"—had long been coveted by the corporate right. Liberal leaders still believed that they knew how to make America a better place, but didn't know how to get there without strong-willed allies in the Democratic Party. Ordinary citizens sympathized with liberalism in the abstract but drifted away with the predictable faithlessness of a baseball fan whose hometown team is in the grip of a losing streak.

The anti-liberal rants of Bush II's hard right provided a perfect contrast to the pre-1980 liberal-dominated Democratic Party. Bush and his wacky band of "neoconservatives" reworked the September 11, 2001 attacks into an excuse to ram through the anti–civil liberties Patriot Act, launch unjustified wars, loot the federal treasury for the benefit of their wealthy contributors and assert a new power to jail or even execute anyone with the stroke of a presidential pen.

And whom do they hate more than anyone? Liberals. Since fear is at the heart of contempt, the cabal that at this writing controls the three branches of the federal government and most state legislatures is obviously terrified that liberalism remains attractive enough to deny them long-lusted-for agenda items.

Which makes me proud.

Win or lose, after all, there's nothing to be ashamed of in the values of tolerance and understanding. In the long run, the alternatives to such basic tenets of decency are so repellant that they're bound to prevail. But there is nothing nobler than the person who fights for what is right even—especially—when conventional wisdom, the powers that be and their sycophants howl that they're stupid and evil and doomed. Joan of Arc, the Polish partisans hung by the Nazis and the four young Freedom Riders murdered in Mississippi all died desperate, abandoned and humiliated. That they were right didn't help them at the time. But it mattered in the long run.

Our situation is not as grim as theirs by a factor of a million, and if one considers the close outcomes of recent elections, it is very nearly peachy-keen. The United States is a nation whose modern history was shaped by liberal values that would be virtually impossible to eradicate. George W. Bush found his limits when he attempted to undermine Social Security. All that's needed now is for liberals to remind Americans of the myriad ways they live better than they would had the conservatives prevailed, to develop a winning platform of ideas for the future and build the infrastructure necessary to sell them to the public. It's hard work, but not nearly as tough a nut to crack as the 12-hour workday. Or women's suffrage. Or civil rights. Or—you get the idea.

Proud to Be a Liberal After Katrina

By Bob Harris

A writer, activist, radio and television star (he's been on *Jeopardy* over a dozen times), Bob Harris's daily political commentary is available at his website, www.bobharris.com.

From the American Heritage dictionary's definition of "liberal":

1a. Not limited to or by established, traditional, orthodox, or authoritarian attitudes, views, or dogmas; free from bigotry.

1b. Favoring proposals for reform, open to new ideas for progress, and tolerant of the ideas and behavior of others; broad-minded.

2a. Tending to give freely; generous: *a liberal benefactor.*

2b. Generous in amount; ample: *a liberal serving of potatoes.*

The dictionary also lists the following as synonyms:

bounteous, bountiful, freehanded, generous, handsome, munificent, openhanded

These adjectives mean willing or marked by a willingness to give unstintingly: *a liberal backer of the arts; a bounteous feast; bountiful compliments; a freehanded host; a generous donation; a handsome offer; a munificent gift; fond and openhanded grandparent*

I am writing this on Thursday, September 1, 2005. America has just suffered the greatest natural disaster in its history, complicated by equally historic failures of planning and leadership.

By now you probably already know the cost of the disaster. At this moment, there is no official count or even estimate of the casualties. The media is simply repeating New Orleans mayor Ray Nagin's guess of "thousands." Watching the disaster unfold across the Gulf Coast, I fear the total number of dead may be much higher. In any case, hundreds of thousands of our fellow citizens have been reduced to refugee status.

By now you probably already know, too, the extent of the incompetence, disregard and deceit involved in Washington's preparation and initial response to the disaster. Funding to maintain the levees was slashed in the last few years, over the repeated screams of New Orleans safety officials and the U.S. Army Corps of Engineers, to help pay for the invasion of Iraq.

As the storm became a Category 5 hurricane, oil rigs were evacuated across the region, but little was done to evacuate the masses of people across the threatened coast who are so poor they lack even the means to leave.

Hours after the floodwalls began to break and water began to flood the city, George W. Bush was at a staged rally for his Medicare agenda, mugging for the camera while playing with a guitar. Last night, as local officials tearfully called for the complete abandonment of an entire American city, Condi Rice attended a Broadway comedy. This morning, while corpses were handled by airport conveyor vehicles on live television, the Secretary of State was still in New York, enjoying Secret Service protection while spending thousands of dollars on Ferragamo shoes.

The head of the Republican National Committee spent this morning sending out an email trying to rally American support not for disaster relief, but for a cut of the estate tax on multimillionaires.

The GOP-controlled Congress, meanwhile, which once held an emergency session on a Sunday night to intervene in the case of Terry Schiavo, has remained on vacation. As things currently stand, they will have done nothing whatsoever until the storm's strike is almost a week old.

The exact scenario that has destroyed so much of New Orleans was considered by FEMA as one of their top-three likely disaster scenarios. But Bush repeatedly appointed FEMA directors with no emergency experience, ignored public warnings from experts that Katrina could cause this exact scenario for at least five days, and then actually went on national television this morning and claimed:

> "I don't think anybody could have anticipated the breach of the levees."

In a bitter irony, George W. Bush's Department of Homeland Security long ago named this very day as the beginning of Disaster Preparedness Month.

So here we are.

Conservatives have been working for over a generation to create the most limited government possible. Their success has led directly to this egregious national failure. If we are to recover, it will be the values of liberalism, on both a personal and policy level, which will begin the healing process.

America now has hundreds of thousands of people in dire need of help. Most of them are poor. Most of them are black. Most of them have never lived in the consumer daydream we too often consider "America." Most of them will need our help not for days, but for months and possibly years. I write this months before you will read this, knowing sadly that even as you do, much work will remain. Helping to rebuild their lives will require all the creativity and imagination and love our hearts and minds can muster. If there has *ever* been a time in the history of this country to respond, proudly, in a liberal fashion—free from bigotry, open to new ideas, tending to give freely and generously in amount—this is surely that time.

Let us now be liberals. America *needs* us to be liberals. Let us give of our time and our means unstintingly. Let us make generous our hearts. Let us make handsome our nation as freehanded hosts. Let us provide for our fellow Americans a bounteous feast. These are the values that are saving lives as I write this, and will be still saving lives, months later, when you read this.

I hope by the time you read this that kindness has overcome cruelty. I hope caring has overcome neglect. I hope, at last, that the values and actions of a liberal people have overcome this unthinkable wrong. But I suspect, watching this tragedy unfold, that there will be much more to be done than I can now even imagine.

So I must be proud to be a liberal in the days to come, not for anything I believe or say or write, but for what I will *do*.

Let us begin. Let us all be liberals.

Proudly.

Our Conservative Friends

By David Rees

David Rees is the author of the cult-hit comic books *Get Your War On*, *My New Fighting Technique Is Unstoppable*, and *My New Filing Technique Is Unstoppable*. His *Get Your War On* comic appears in every issue of *Rolling Stone*.

OUR CONSERVATIVE FRIENDS

Can you believe those liberals? Goddamn them! Everything would work out fine if they would just sit down and stop *screaming* all the time! *Jesus, grow up already!*

It's like they're cut off from reality! They don't understand how the world *really* works, so they jump around and scream like children! *They're unhinged, man! GOD!* IT MAKES ME WANT TO—

Umm... You should lower your voice. You're kind of yelling.

Warning Labels

The Word "Liberal"

By Eric Alterman

Eric Alterman is Professor of English at Brooklyn College of the City University of New York, media columnist for *The Nation*, the "Altercation" weblogger for MSNBC.com, and a senior fellow at the Center for American Progress, where he writes and edits the "Think Again" column. He is also the author of the bestsellers *What Liberal Media? The Truth About Bias and the News* and *The Book on Bush: How George W. (Mis)leads America* (with Mark Green) and *When Presidents Lie: A History of Deception and Its Consequences*.

What do our opponents mean when they apply to us the label "Liberal?" If by "Liberal" they mean, as they want people to believe, someone who is soft in his policies abroad, who is against local government, and who is unconcerned with the taxpayer's dollar, then . . . we are not that kind of "Liberal." But if by a "Liberal" they mean someone who looks ahead and not behind, someone who welcomes new ideas without rigid reactions, someone who cares about the welfare of the people—their health, their housing, their schools, their jobs, their civil rights, and their civil liberties—someone who believes we can break through the stalemate and suspicions that grip us in our policies abroad, if that is what they mean by a "Liberal," then I'm proud to say I'm a "Liberal."

—John F. Kennedy, September 14, 1960

Judging merely by the titles that pop up on a search of Amazon.com, calling a person a "liberal" in contemporary America is barely a step up from axe-murderer or pedophile. They range from Ann Coulter's *How to Talk to a Liberal (If You Must)*; Michael Savage's *The Savage Nation: Saving America from the Liberal Assault on Our Borders, Language and Culture* and *Liberalism Is a Mental Disorder*; Mona Charen's *Useful Idiots: How Liberals Got It Wrong in the Cold War and Still Blame America First*; David Limbaugh's *Persecution: How Liberals Are Waging War Against Christianity*; Sean Hannity's *Let Freedom Ring:*

Winning the War of Liberty over Liberalism; James Patterson's *Reckless Disregard: How Liberal Democrats Undercut Our Military, Endanger Our Soldiers, and Jeopardize Our Security*, and so on. Also available at Amazon are bumper stickers reading: "Liberalism Is A Disease," "Liberalism Is Not a Family Value," and "If Ignorance Is Bliss, Then Liberalism Must Be Nirvana."

Of course the real problem is that these titles represent a kind of consensus on the right and in much of mainstream media. When Rush Limbaugh returned to the airwaves on November 17, 2003, he admitted to his 15-20 million listeners that while he may be "powerless" to overcome his drug addiction without professional help, he would not, he promised, turn into "a linguini-spined liberal." The national media, alleged by all to be infested by closet liberals, reported these insults verbatim, as if to be so obvious that they were undeserving of refutation or even reply.

At first blush this is odd. After all, 52 percent of Americans told Gallup pollsters that they "didn't respect Limbaugh now and never did," putting them, no doubt, in the "linguini-spined" category. In recent times, much of the mainstream media have incorporated many of these same attitudes, if not their occasionally obscene terminology. Liberalism is something from which savvy politicians must run—or perhaps hide under the bed, at least until the guests have gone home.

Ever since George McGovern was defeated in 1972 with the help of the criminal conspiracy that was Richard Nixon's reelection campaign, the media has made a sport of bashing liberals come election time. As Michael Kinsley pointed out during the 2004 election, "It's true enough that this is a moment when the Democrats are called upon to reject extreme liberalism (whatever that might be) and to embrace moderation. But that is only because every moment is such a moment. The opinion that the

Democrats need to foreswear McGovernism and prove their commitment to moderation is one of the very safest in all of punditry." Yet Republicans, Kinsley notes, receive the equivalent of a free ideological pass regardless of the fact that they are led by two men whose political extremism has no analogy in power circles in the other party. And the Republicans are under no pressure to avoid the word "conservative."

The demonization of the word "liberal" has been an ongoing project of the well-funded right and draws its fire from intellectuals who should really know better. Shelby Steele, for instance, has provided useful and interesting challenges to conventional wisdom on race and affirmative action, but look what he wrote on the *Wall Street Journal*'s editorial page about John Walker Lindh and liberals. Speaking of the allegedly liberal values of Marin County, California, where Lindh was raised, and taking a page from the playbook of former Republican House Speaker Newt Gingrich, Steele charged, sans evidence, that "This liberalism thrives as a subversive, winking, countercultural hipness. . . . Cultural liberalism serves up American self-hate to the young as idealism. It's too much to say that treason is a rite of passage in this context. But that is exactly how it turned out for Walker. In radical Islam he found both the victim's authority and the hatred of America that had been held out to him as marks of authenticity. . . . And when he turned on his country to be secure in his new faith, he followed a logic that was a part of his country's culture."

This raises the question, why does Shelby Steele hate America? An interesting line of reasoning, this, considering that conservatives normally reject victimization in favor of personal responsibility. Apparently, liberalism trumps free will in Steele's sociological methodology.

One can discern few, if any, limits to the kinds of accusations to which prominent conservatives have attached to liberals in recent years. At a May 2005 dinner in honor of the now former House Majority Leader Tom DeLay, speaker after speaker assailed what conservative commentator Phyllis Schlafly termed "hysterical paranoid liberals." Among DeLay's most dedicated supporters was the Reverend Billy James Hargis, who denounced liberalism as "double-standard, Satanic hypocrisy." (A sex scandal lost Hargis his ministry in 1976.)[1] A spokesperson for the conservative Club for Growth termed supporters of the liberal Howard Dean presidential candidacy to be "a tax-hiking, government-expanding, latte-drinking, sushi-eating, Volvo-driving, New York Times-reading, body-piercing, Hollywood-loving, left-wing freak show."[2]

This kind of trash talking is hardly limited to the more extreme fringes of American politics. Former Republican House Majority Leader Dick Armey wrote in 1995 that the New Deal and Great Society on the one hand and the Five-Year Plan and Great Leap Forward on the other were created by "the same sort of person," the only differences between them being those of "power and nerve."[3] Senator Rick Santorum of Pennsylvania, the third-ranking Republican in the Senate, blamed the city of Boston's history of "liberalism" for the Roman Catholic Church's pedophile scandal, saying that the city's "sexual license" and "sexual freedom" nurtured an environment that gave rise to the molestation of children by priests. "It is no surprise that Boston, a seat of academic, political, and cultural liberalism in America, lies at the center of the storm" of the clergy's sexual-abuse scandal, he said.[4] And Janice Rogers Brown, confirmed in June 2005 to the federal appeals court in Washington, DC, following a lengthy Senate battle, has termed the New Deal to be "the triumph of our socialist revolution." "In the heyday of liberal democracy," she argued, "all roads lead to slavery."[5]

Ann Coulter, whom fellow right-winger Jonah Goldberg once called "barely coherent," adding that in one *National Review* column (which the magazine refused to publish and ultimately led to her departure) she was guilty of "emoting rather than thinking, and badly needing editing and some self-censorship, or what is commonly referred to as 'judgment.'" Her book, *Treason*, took liberalism to task for just about everything, from "undermining victory in the Cold War," saying that by "[b]etraying the manifest national defense objectives of the country . . . [liberals] aim to destroy America from the inside with their relentless attacks on morality and the truth." The problem with her "reasoning," of course, stems from the fact that without the Democratic-controlled Congress of the Cold War years, none of those large defense appropriation bills would have been passed. But no matter. She continues, "Whether they are defending the Soviet Union or bleating for Saddam Hussein, liberals are always against America."

And yet despite all of the above—as well as her joking about how lovely it would be if terrorists blew up the *New York Times*—she was rewarded by *USA Today* with a column covering the 2004 Democratic National Convention, until she turned in her unreadable personal attacks on the physical appearances of the delegates and *USA Today* suddenly decided that hiring her was not such a brilliant idea after all. And even after that, she was graced with a loving cover story in *Time* magazine in which a love-struck journalist named John Cloud endorsed the accuracy of her writings after what he admitted was a casual Google search.

Even so, all this works. As Princeton professor Paul Starr notes, "The use of the vocabulary of treason is a measure of how thoroughly conservatives have transferred the passions of anti-communism into an internal war against those whom they think of as the enemies of American culture and values. And these were, as I recall from the 1960s, the same people who decried the loss of civility."

Given the rhetorical dominance of conservatives over the past several decades, one might be surprised to learn from a June 2005 *Wall Street Journal* analysis that "[The] proportion of Americans calling themselves "liberal" edged up to 21 percent in [pollster Stan] Greenberg's May poll from 16 percent a month earlier. Self-identified "conservatives" dropped to 37 percent from 41 percent. And why not? One of the most honored guests at the Democratic Convention in 2004 turned out to be none other than George McGovern. As he told a reporter from *National Journal* when queried about his apparently alien ideological affiliation, "Every program that ever helped working people—from rural electrification to Medicare—was enacted by liberals over the opposition of conservatives. When people tell me they don't like liberals, I ask, 'Do you like Social Security? If so, then shut up!'"

Notes

1. Richard Hofstadter, *The Paranoid Style in American Politics* (Cambridge: Harvard University Press, 1996) 140. (Chapter 7, note 5)

2. Barbara Ehrenrich, "Dude, Where's That Elite?," *New York Times*, 1 July 2004, sec A, p. 21.

3.Richard K. Armey, *The Freedom Revolution: The New Republican House Majority Leader Tells Why Big Government Failed, Why Freedom Works, and How We Will Rebuild America* (Washington: Regnery, 1995), 16. (Chapter 3, note 30)

4. Susan Milligan, "Santorum resolute on Boston rebuke, insists liberalism set stage for abuse," *Boston Globe*, July 13, 2005

5. David D. Kirkpatrick, "Women in the News: Seeing Slavery in Liberalism—Janice Rogers Brown," *New York Times*, 9 June 2005, sec A, P. 22.

Why I Am Not a Progressive

By Bill Scher

Bill Scher is the executive editor of LiberalOasis.com and a weekly contributor to Air America Radio's evening program "The Majority Report." His first book, *Wait! Don't Move to Canada!* will be published by Rodale in the fall of 2006.

---

*Call me a conservative. . . . I'm proud of it. I vote that way.
. . . Is there anybody in the Senate who will admit to being
liberal?*

—Sen. Lindsey Graham (R-SC), July 11, 2004,
ABC's *This Week with George Stephanopoulos*

When a group of liberal Democratic House members (and one
independent) decided in 1991 to form a caucus to increase their
influence on the direction of the party, they did not call it the
Liberal Caucus, choosing instead to call it the Progressive Caucus. Why reject the most obvious title? Because to be known as a
"liberal" is the adult equivalent of having cooties, and to call
yourself a "progressive" is akin to getting a cootie shot.

The problem is, as any eight-year old with a chronic case of
cooties eventually figures out, that there is no such thing as a
cootie shot. Thus, the attempt by liberals to inoculate themselves
with a "progressive" injection has been a clear failure.

To be fair to the "progressives," there is superficial logic in
their strategy. Since the Harris poll began asking Americans
about their ideological tendencies in the late 1960s, only about
20 percent of Americans have called themselves "liberal." So, the
logic goes, since it's just a mere label, why stick with a loser?

However, as linguist George Lakoff can tell you, words
evoke "frames." He titled his book *Don't Think of an Elephant* to
illustrate just that point. Once somebody says to you, "don't
think of an elephant," you surely will think of an elephant. The

word itself automatically triggers something in your head, and the attributes that make up the frame—"large," "gray" and "trunk"—are instantly conjured up.

The word "liberal" conjures up its own frame. And considering how few Americans are willing to call themselves liberal, it's likely that many of the word's attributes are the ones that conservatives have sought to pin on it—irresponsible, soft, permissive, weak, elitist and immoral. But when you use the word "progressive," progress, advancement, moving forward and success are the kind of inoffensive attributes that can be expected to pop into people's minds.

And so the switch to the less controversial "progressive" was made. Not since Gov. Michael Dukakis, in a desperate move nine days before the 1988 presidential election, dared to say, "Yes, I am a liberal" (after months of evasion and denials) has any Democrat of note fully embraced the label. But while ditching "liberal" might have made some sense 17-plus years ago, we all should realize by now that shaking off an ideological label is not so easy.

For better or for worse, "liberal" and "conservative" are part of the American political lexicon, and the mainstream media reflexively uses those terms to define our ideological spectrum. Political reporters regularly refer to seemingly large groups of "liberal" Democratic senators even though not a single senator openly defines himself or herself that way, not to mention most House members and prominent activists.

And fear of the "liberal" tag is like blood in the water for the conservative sharks. Without anyone with an interest in liberalism defending and defining the ideology's natural label, it's easier for Republicans to twist and defile "liberal" into a potent, all-purpose slur.

But despite the pounding "liberal" has taken from Republicans, the solution is not to run further away from the word. That only makes the problem worse.

For example, look at how John Kerry and John Edwards addressed questions about being "liberal" during the 2004 presidential campaign. Instead of challenging the word's negative connotations, they sought to lament the use of ideological labels in general, while trying to pivot toward the political center.

In October 2004, when Edwards was asked by ABC News' Ted Koppel, "Are you a liberal?" he responded:

"No. I don't believe in labels, first of all. I don't believe they mean anything. I think what John Kerry and I are mainstream America."

Kerry, asked a similar question a week later by NBC's Tom Brokaw, responded similarly:

"It depends on what the issue is, Tom. I've always hated labels and I don't abide by labels."

Such statements imply that being a liberal is something despicable. We are effectively saying to the country, "What I am is a bad thing. I am most definitely in the minority and I always will be. Why would you want to join me in my shame? Why would you let your kids come near me? I can't even bear to look you in the eye and tell you what I really am."

In defense of Kerry and Edwards, one could not have expected them to suddenly embrace the "liberal" label so late in the campaign. Since the word has been consciously left unprotected for so long, you can't just pick it back up, all bloodied and bruised, and expect to get anywhere with it. It has to be constantly defined, defended, modernized and marketed because, if you don't define your own labels, someone's going to define them for you.

As much as we may dislike labels, we can't dismiss them. We can sniff at the simplistic nature of our political discourse, but every politician needs to sum up his or her general approach to government in some basic way. That's how voters get a sense of what they're voting for. Until we can scrub off the stigma attached to the word "liberal," Americans won't be comfortable with the direction in which Democrats would take the country.

Unfortunately, there's no single catch phrase, no one book, no snappy ad, that's going to quickly turn things around. It will take years and require long-term thinking and a whole lot of patience and tenacity.

However, political leaders tend not to think past the next election. So don't expect Harry Reid, Nancy Pelosi, Howard Dean or any of the prospective presidential candidates in 2008 to take the lead in revitalizing "liberal." Like many things in the decentralized Democratic Party, change will have to come from the grassroots on up.

By taking to the airwaves, the letters page and the blogs, we can take the lead in re-associating "liberal" with the values and beliefs that speak to Americans' struggles and desires in an insecure economy and a destabilized world: responsive government, sound management, shared responsibility, personal freedom and the spread of liberty and prosperity, not destruction and hypocrisy, across the globe.

But while change will likely begin with us on the ground, it certainly couldn't hurt if the House Progressive Caucus changed its name.

The Sensible Liberal

By Tom Tomorrow

Tom Tomorrow is the creator of the widely syndicated political cartoon *This Modern World*, and a two-time winner of the Robert F. Kennedy Memorial Journalism Award. His blog can be read at www.thismodernworld.com.

THIS MODERN WORLD

by TOM TOMORROW

HE'S NOT JUST A *LIBERAL*--HE'S A

SENSIBLE LIBERAL!

MODERATION IN PURSUIT OF FURTHER MODERATION IS *NO VICE!*

IN THE RUNUP TO WAR, HE CAREFULLY CONSIDERED *ALL SIDES* OF THE *ISSUE.*

GIVEN THE *UNDENIABLE THREAT* POSED BY SADDAM, I FEEL I *MUST* SUPPORT THE WAR!

IT'S THE *SENSIBLE* THING TO DO!

EVEN NOW, HE VIEWS THE ANTI-WAR PROTESTERS WITH *DISDAIN.*

OKAY, SURE, THEY WERE RIGHT AND I WAS WRONG--

--BUT THEY WEREN'T AS *SENSIBLE* AS ME!

OUTSPOKEN CRITICS OF THE ADMINISTRATION MAKE HIM *VERY UNCOMFORTABLE.*

IS IT *REALLY* NECESSARY TO CALL THE PRESIDENT A "*LIAR*"?

I SHOULD THINK IT WOULD SUFFICE TO GENTLY SUGGEST THAT HE *MAY* BE SOMEWHAT *MISGUIDED!*

HE'S *PARTICULARLY* QUICK TO DISTANCE HIMSELF FROM *MICHAEL MOORE.*

I THINK HIS TACTICS ARE *BAD FOR DEMOCRACY!*

DOESN'T HE *UNDERSTAND?* THE *BEST* WAY TO REACH AMERICANS IS THROUGH *PONDEROUS ESSAYS* IN *OBSCURE POLITICAL JOURNALS!*

YES, HE'S A *SENSIBLE* LIBERAL-- HAVE YOU *HEARD?* BUSH WANTS TO SUSPEND THE *CONSTITUTION* AND DECLARE HIMSELF *DICTATOR-FOR-LIFE!*

WELL THEN--WE NEED TO CONSIDER HIS PROPOSAL ON ITS *MERITS*-- SO WE CAN REACH A *SENSIBLE* CONCLUSION!

--AND HE HAS THE GRATITUDE OF *REPUBLICANS EVERYWHERE.*

TOM TOMORROW©2004... www.thismodernworld.com

Acting Locally, Thinking Globally

Mr. Pollack's Neighborhood

By Neal Pollack

Neal Pollack's parenting memoir, *Alternadad*, will be published in 2006 by Pantheon Books. He lives in Los Angeles with his family.

One Friday night around 11 p.m., as I was sitting in my dark-blue leather recliner happily watching my NetFlix DVD of *Dirty Pretty Things,* I heard some noises outside. I looked out my window. Two guys were kicking the crap out of another guy on my front lawn. There was a white Cadillac parked at the curb. A woman got out.

"Ramon!" she yelled. "I told you to leave him alone. He didn't do nothing!"

The victim got up and stumbled further into my yard, dragging his left side. His assailants followed, knocked him over, and resumed booting him in the kidneys. At this point, I opened the window.

"Get off my fucking lawn, goddammit!" I screamed.

They looked up for a second, and then started into the guy again. Eventually, he rolled away from them across my lawn until he was directly under my two-year-old son's bedroom window. "I'm calling the cops!" I shouted out the window.

By the time the cops arrived, there was no one around for them to arrest. I explained to them that the white Cadillac often idled on the street corner. Sometimes women would get out and walk down the street toward the apartment complex two blocks away. Sometimes men would get into the car and it would drive away and then, a few hours later, it would return to pick up the women who were getting off their shift. The cops said they'd look into the situation.

It's never been my habit to disrupt the activities of a small business, particularly one that's locally based. But I've also always had a maxim: If three guys are fighting over a hooker under your son's bedroom window, then it's time to clean up the neighborhood.

So that's what I tried to do.

My wife and I didn't move to Austin, Texas, to get away from the problems of a big city, precisely, but we also didn't expect to find them here. We knew that the neighborhood, Harmon Triangle, where we'd chosen to buy a house was across the highway from the site of the old municipal airport, and that the old airport site was about to undergo a big "mixed-use" redevelopment, including a children's hospital. This would cause a boom in our property values. However, our realtor had neglected to tell us a few other things.

The neighborhood had been home, until quite recently, to the Rio Motel and the associated Club Rio, which in 1999, Texas State Attorney General John Cornyn had called "a haven for illegal criminal activity." The motel had once been a Best Western, until it became Club Rio sometime in the 1980s. By the time it closed, it had been home to the capture of a murder suspect, several crack busts, a lot of gun complaints, more than 300 arrests and a rash of bloody mattresses tossed into the alley. The neighborhood behind the motel—the one I later moved to—played host to wasted partiers and drug addicts, who wandered the streets all night long.

However, the problems with Club Rio were considered over by the time we arrived. The motel was by then in the hands of a responsible owner, and no one in the neighborhood complained about it anymore. But they did spend a lot of time complaining about the First Workers' Day Labor Center. Soon after the closing of the Rio, the city announced that the center would move from downtown into the neighborhood where I would later buy property. This would be Austin's only official day-labor outlet. Since Austin widely enjoys a reputation as an "amnesty" city for illegal immigrants, it would become the most popular one in the state.

The Harmon Triangle had always been considered a way station to the airport, so it had never had much political representation. But now a neighborhood association was formed for the least noble of reasons: to oppose the center, and specifically to oppose illegal immigration. It unappealingly called itself the Eye-35 Neighbors Association, because it was located near I-35.

The leader of the association was a man named Fred Dupuy, who happened to belong to a group called Texans for Fair Immigration. He also hosted a weekly Tuesday-night anti-immigrant cable-access show. After the moving of the day-labor site was announced, he took to showing up at city-council meetings to protest, doing such politically subtle things as wearing a toilet seat around his neck and saying, "Our neighborhood is going down the toilet." For obvious reasons, the city did not heed his warnings.

When the city opened the day-labor site, Dupuy ran protests outside the building, brandishing signs that read, among other things, "Notice: Employing Illegal Aliens Is a Violation of Federal Law." The irony of the whole situation was that the workers didn't want the day-labor site located there either, because it was too far away from where most of them lived, and there were no good bus routes nearby. This made people doubly sympathetic to their cause. A documentary was even made about the "struggle" to open the day-labor center, called *Los Trabajadores*. The movie aired on PBS in the spring of 2002. If I'd been watching TV then, I might not have moved to that particular spot five months later.

By the time Regina and I arrived in the neighborhood, Fred Dupuy had left, though his cable-access show lived on. There were few signs of conflict or danger. Our street comprised wood-frame houses built in the 1940s. They were all between 800 and 1500 square feet, and most of them were in good condition. All our neighbors were warm and friendly and welcoming. It seemed like we had found a peaceful little patch.

Two weeks after we moved in, we went to a meeting at the community church down the street. It was attended by ten people and presided over by the only remaining officer of the Eye-35 Neighbors Association, a tired and nervous woman about our age who, as it turned out, lived across the street from us. The first agenda item came up.

"We're thinking of having a lawyer write a letter," she said.

"To whom?" I said. "About what?"

"We want to threaten the residents of the apartment down the street," she said. "If they think the INS is coming, maybe they'll stop patronizing the Day Labor Center."

Regina and I looked at each other. "What Day Labor Center?" I said.

That's when I got the story, with special emphasis on how poorly the city had treated the neighborhood. While the xenophobia of years past still lingered a bit, it was obvious that no one really bought into it anymore. Still, I was a neighbor now, so I felt the need to take a stand.

"I don't know about the rest of you," I said. "But I'm a liberal. And I am *not* going to be party to calling the INS on my neighbors."

Seven of the ten people at the meeting actually agreed with me. It broke up soon after. That was the last-ever meeting of the Eye-35 Neighbors Association.

On our walk home, Regina said, "What the hell kind of a neighborhood did we move into?"

A few weeks later, Regina gave birth to our son, and we suddenly had bigger concerns than neighborhood politics. But the neighborhood's problems existed whether we were new parents or not. Soon enough I, an ordinary citizen and father of one, would be forced into politics for the most basic and self-interested reason—to protect my family.

Across the street from us there is a little house. On the day we moved in, we saw a bunch of dudes hanging out on the front porch drinking beer. They were pretty noisy. But I found it charming. People! Drinking beer! On a porch! In Texas! It was just like *King of the Hill.*

As the months crept along, however, the little house grew less charming. We got to know the people who lived next to the house, who had a son about a year older than ours. Little Eamon was always asking his parents when the "scary men" were going to go away. They had to put up a bamboo fence because they were tired of watching people shit in the backyard next door. That's probably because the house next door no longer had plumbing or electricity.

The house's official occupant was an alcoholic Vietnam veteran named Al, whose parents had once owned the place but were long gone. The deed now belonged to Al's nephew, who lived in Colorado. Al, who looked vaguely like the actor Richard Farnsworth from *The Grey Fox,* had been an habitué of Club Rio, and much of that club's culture had migrated to his house. Women came in and out at all hours. There were always cars pulling up to the house, and, of course, there was the ubiquitous white Cadillac.

Early one evening, I was in the back of our house pretending to work when Regina came barging in.

"Something crazy is going on at Al's house," she said. "These four women just pulled up in a car."

"This goddamn neighborhood," I said.

I looked out the front window. These women were on Al's lawn, screaming at him. Then one of them picked up a white metal porch chair and hurled it at him. A geyser of blood spurted from Al's forehead.

"Good Lord!" I said.

My next-door neighbor Scott, a semiprofessional weightlifter whom I'd never seen lose his temper, then came roaring out of his house waving a silver-played .38 special. He charged across the street, gun in the air.

"Get the hell out of my neighborhood," he said. "NOW!"

"Call the cops," I said to Regina.

By the time the cops got here, the situation was over. The women had left. All the cops did was lecture Scott, who sat sheepishly on the curb, not the least because his wife was making relentless fun of him.

"Who do you think you are?" she said. "Michael Douglas?"

Still, it didn't seem right to me that we had to live in the middle of all this crap, and that my taxpaying neighbor, who'd bought into the neighborhood when jets still roared overhead eighteen hours a day and Rio Motel crackheads parked their cars in front of his house, was the one getting in trouble with the cops. It was time to take political action.

The next day, I went to see my neighbor Jennings, the one who lived next door to Al's house.

"It doesn't have to be like this," I said. I'd seen neighborhood groups in Chicago work with the police with some success. It hadn't worked so well in Philadelphia when I'd lived there, but this place wasn't as dangerous as Philadelphia. Then again, if all you can say about your neighborhood is that it's not as bad as Philly, then you're using the wrong scale of comparison.

Since the heyday of Fred Dupuy, no one in the Harmon Triangle had dared attempt anything political. But I had the naively progressive idea that things could get done. After all, I'd met our state representative at the Texas Book Festival a couple of years before.

I made an appointment with him, and Jennings and I went down to the capital. We told Representative Nashtiat, a lefty New York Jew adrift in the Texas House, our problems. I guess he had some power, because the next day I got a call from our "district representative" at the Austin Police Department.

"You should come to us if you have problems," he said.

"Well," I said. "We're here now. Help us."

A week later, ten of my neighbors were in my living room, along with two representatives of the APD. Our district rep was a square-jawed linebacker named Crumrine. I had this feeling that he would be able to get things done.

We filled the cops in on the specifics of our neighborhood problem. I told them that we'd been given a bad rap in the past, but that things were different now. This wasn't an anti-immigrant gambit. No one, immigrant or native, wants a dangerous abandoned house on the block.

The police gave us a bunch of fliers and pamphlets and other police effluvia. Most important, they gave us their business cards. But they declined my offer of a Shiner Bock. "You call us if anything happens," said Officer Crumrine.

I saw my opportunity a week later. One morning I looked out my window and saw a little girl playing in an abandoned shopping cart. She was school-aged, and this was the middle of a school day. I called the police. They showed up fifteen minutes later.

Turned out, this girl and her sister were living in the house with their mother and two dozen other people. The mother turned tricks on a dirty mattress in the back bedroom. The police called Children and Family Services. A case was opened on the mother. She got to keep the kids, on the conditions that she'd put them in school and that she'd get her own apartment.

Over the next month, my neighbors and I called the cops every day. We eventually got the house condemned. That didn't stop people from living there, but their time was borrowed. The police contacted Al's nephew and told him that he'd better sell the house now. You don't get any money if the county seizes your property.

The house went on the market. One morning, we saw Al loading his belongings into a pickup truck. I went over to talk to him.

"I'm sorry about this," I said.

"It's a relief," he said. "These people were killing me."

"What's happening now with you?"

"They got me a room at a nursing home," he said. "There's a smoking lounge and I'll have my own shower. It's been a long time since I've had three meals a day."

"Right on," I said.

That night, a half dozen people tried to slip into Al's house through the back door. Jennings called the cops on them. They didn't come back. A few days later, a tow truck came and pulled an abandoned pickup out of the driveway. There was a man sleeping in it. A few days later, he returned with the car and told Jennings, "You'll never get rid of us."

That was the last time we saw him.

Our work in taking down Al's house had drawn the attention of the Ridgetop/Morningside Neighborhood Association, which was directly to the north of us, across a busy street. They'd been around for two decades and their officers worked for either environmental organizations or in the child-welfare industry. They were decent people who wanted their neighborhoods safe and their property values to rise, but weren't anti-immigrant mercenary jerks. They incorporated the Harmon Triangle into their fold, and immediately their job got a lot harder. But at least now we had real representation with real contacts at City Hall. I was elected co-vice-president of the neighborhood association for the Harmon Triangle sector. This wasn't exactly what I wanted on my business card.

Probably the best thing about our neighborhood was this old shack called Mrs. Johnson's Donuts, which had been open since 1948. Compared to Mrs. Johnson's product, Krispy Kremes tasted like stale NutterButters. Every night starting at nine, I could smell the products of Mrs. Johnson (who was, as far as I could tell, a middle-aged man from India) from my back porch. I wanted to rename the neighborhood Donut Town, and I wanted to be the mayor of Donut Town, instead of vice president of the Harmon Triangle sector. But that remained a fantasy. We had real-world concerns.

Seems that the problems in our neighborhood weren't limited to just Al's now former house. The bad news had now moved to three apartment buildings down the street from me, which festered with crime. The police started putting heat on the various owners by calling inspectors and running drug stings. One of the buildings was placed in receivership and became a 43-unit squat, a dark, filthy place with no electricity or running water.

One day, however, I drove by and all the cars were gone from the parking lot. Signs of construction began appearing. An "under new management" banner went up. Then all of a sudden, a nice wooden sign appeared, informing us that the building was now called The Montecito. I pulled into the parking lot and met the new owner. They'd just begun rehabbing. The place hardly looked spectacular, but it was clean. He'd be renting, he said, at $500 for a one-bedroom and $600 for a two-bedroom, pretty much the going rate for a basic Austin apartment. Plus he'd be screening tenants.

The second building had new management as well, focusing on renting to immigrant families. They held a holiday party for the kids, and a building-wide yard sale. A job fair was in the works. The police threw something called "Operation Cooperation." Management made sure that parents got to know the principal at the local elementary school.

That left the third building, "The Highland," which housed, in twenty-eight units, every last scumbag in the neighborhood.

One afternoon, I walked down to the Shamrock station for a Diet Cherry Coke, as was my wont, stopping along the way to talk to a neighbor about how great it was that crime was finally down in the neighborhood.

On the way back from the store, I ran into Little Eamon's mother.

"I went to pick Eamon up at school," she said. "And on the way home, I tried to drive down Harmon. There were all kinds of police cars and they'd blocked off the street with yellow tape."

"That sounds like a murder scene," I said. "I worked as a reporter for years, so I know. Plus, I watch a lot of TV."

I took a two-block stroll toward the yellow caution plastic. There must have been a dozen police cars. A few people were milling around.

"What happened?" I said.

Here's what I learned: The dead guy had been twenty-two. He'd come out of the building to defend his father, who was in a fight over a woman, and two guys brained him with a shovel. The woman then ran into her apartment, came out with an unraveled coat hanger, and stabbed the guy in the heart until he died.

This moment had been coming. The previous two weeks had been menacing ones. Large groups of drunks, shirtless if the weather were nice, stood on the sidewalk, glowering at passing cars. Late in the afternoon, they started standing in the middle of the road and staring at cars that went by in a perverse game of chicken. It looked like one of them might snap at any moment, or at least throw one of their 40-oz. Budweisers at a windshield. It was, as I said on every local newscast that night, only a matter of time before someone got killed.

At the crime scene, I walked around looking for a sympathetic face. The poor guy at the rental house across the street was trembling, saying that he was going to break his lease. The rest of the people standing around were residents of the Highland or of Hidden Vines, all of whom were saying that they had to get out, and were telling the TV cameras that this was a crime-infested shithole.

I knew that something had to be done immediately to save our neighborhood's reputation. I went home and popped off this email to the association officers:

From: Neal Pollack
Subject: Murder on Harmon Avenue

Hi Everyone:
You read that right. Today at approximately 2 p.m., someone was murdered in the middle of Harmon

Avenue in front of the Hillside Apartments. The police have no one in custody.

This is a disaster, and a tragedy. The APD, the city and any real-estate powers-that-be need to come together, now, and stop the senseless crime and brutality that has plagued this neighborhood for too long. I humbly request that we put the other issues on the back burner temporarily and unite as a neighborhood association to put some heat on, and I need ideas about what we should do.

We need the managers of the apartments at our next meeting. We need the APD there. And we need a representative from the city there, in some capacity.

I spoke to the media at the crime scene, and told them that this was a chronic problem that hurts everyone in the neighborhood, homeowner and renter, naturalized citizen and immigrant, and families of all income levels. If we come at this problem from the left, as opposed to the right, like the previous administration did, we might have some success . . . We need to meet with politicians and developers and police officials. And we need to organize people in this neighborhood now, to have a Harmon Triangle–only (plus other neighborhood officers) meeting at the church on Harmon. This is serious, and this cannot stand.

The neighborhood association responded quickly, and with outrage, firing off letters to our district police representative, throwing ideas out about who to call and who to bring into the coalition.

But I was at the hot center of this one. My co-VP for the

area was out of town. I was the only guy on the ground. My first action was to write a letter, which I copied at OfficeMax and distributed, with some help, on Saturday morning. It went:

Dear Neighbors:

My name is Neal Pollack. I'm a vice-president, representing the Harmon Triangle area, of the Ridgetop Neighborhood Association. And I'm writing to let you know that we're all stunned and saddened by the tragic murder that occurred on the 4700 block of Harmon Avenue on Wednesday.

But I'm also writing to let you know that we understand, from discussions with the Austin Police Department, that this was an isolated incident, a personal argument gone terribly wrong. Over the last several months, the Austin Police Department, in conjunction with neighbors, has been working very hard to improve the crime situation and living conditions in this neighborhood, with great efficiency and great success. The crime that happened on Wednesday was extremely unfortunate, but it was also the kind of crime that could have happened anywhere in the city.

This neighborhood has had problems in the past. But we are working to change this and have made significant progress. With the redevelopment of the old airport across the street, new home construction everywhere, and new businesses opening up on Airport Boulevard, the possibilities and realities of change have never been brighter in the Harmon Triangle. Recently, our area became a part of the larger Ridgetop Neighborhood Association, an established, well-organized group that will work hard to represent our interests to the city. We will be isolated and forgotten no more.

But we still have more work to do, and we need your help. We must use this sad incident as an opportunity to build a stronger, safer neighborhood. We'll hold a community meeting within the next 10 days or so with the neighborhood association and with representatives from the APD, where we can discuss the situation in greater detail. I encourage you to come, and to help make this a better neighborhood for all of us.

A few of us met at my house the night after the murder and decided to take a three-pronged approach. One, we'd work with the police to get the bad apartments shut down. Based on previous experience, I was confident we'd accomplish this goal within a month. Two, we had to build a broad organization of people who could form a real neighborhood association. We had to mix homeowners and renters, storeowners and retail property owners, school officials, apartment managers, and so on. Everyone had to have an interest in making this a nice neighborhood. Third, we had to start doing long-term political work, hooking up with state officials and local officials and big-time developers, so we could use this incident as a catalyst to *really* remake the neighborhood. I was going to turn this into something positive!

Most of all, I was going to try to bring the families from the apartment buildings into the fold. I received a letter from the principal at the neighborhood school. It went, in part:

As we've met with parents we've found out that there are prostitutes that frequent (and some may even live in) the apartments because there are a lot of single men that live there. Our students that live there say that the police come by frequently because of brawls that break out due to the drinking. Some of the moms have expressed concerns at our parent breakfasts saying that they have been threatened when they try to seek help from the authorities. The managers and the owners are trying to remodel the complexes and this is good. However, the children that do live there are in harm's way daily when they go home. School is their safe haven and many treasure the days when we have after-school programs for them because they don't have to go home right away. Some of the parents say that drugs have been offered to their children and it's difficult for them to let their children go outside to play after 5 p.m. on most days because of what might be going on outside. One of the parents has to move because of the harassment she puts up with from drunk men who may not even live in the apartment complex. She's a single parent with four small children. There's a good group of parents who want to help find a solution to this problem because it's in their best interest to make the apartments safer for the children.

The problems were far worse than I'd known.

That night, my wife rubbed my shoulders and said, "You're a good man." Three years previous, I might have replied, "Don't I know it?" But this time, I just patted her hand and said, "I'm just doing what I have to for our son." And I was sincere.

The neighborhood quieted down after that. We finally persuaded the police that things were bad enough that they had to establish a permanent office in the neighborhood, so they took over one of the apartments in the Montecito building. There were still the usual burglary and car-stereo-theft complaints, but those are endemic to every urban neighborhood. However, the overwhelming problems seemed to have gone away. Or so I thought.

I was peacefully sitting in my lounge chair on a Saturday night, watching Montgomery Clift and Elizabeth Taylor in *A Place in the Sun*. Suddenly, from outside, I heard a booming bass from a car stereo. This was common in the neighborhood. But this time, it didn't go away. So I looked through the curtains. A guy got out of the passenger seat of the car, stepped onto my neighbor's lawn, threw something on the grass, and stood there yelling at it.

"What the hell?" I said.

I ran outside, in my T-shirt and boxer briefs, and down my front walk, getting close enough so that I could see the license plate.

"Write this down!" I said, relaying the plate number to Regina.

"I don't have a pen!" she said.

"Hurry, or I won't remember it!" I said. "Where's our flashlight?"

I went back inside, put on a pair of sweatpants, but no shoes, and walked out into the dark, onto my neighbor's lawn. I'd taken three steps in the grass when I felt something soft underfoot, heard a little "eep" sound, and felt something nip my big toe.

I went back to my front porch, where Regina was waiting in her bathrobe.

"What happened?" she said.

"I got bit," I said.

"You got *bit*?" she said.

"Yeah," I said. "Something bit me."

She had the flashlight, and we went back across the street,

more carefully this time. We shined it around, and there sat a terrified-looking rat. Regina poked it with a stick to make sure it was alive, and it ran away.

"That rat could have rabies," she said.

"Well, that's just great," I replied.

I called 311 while Regina swabbed my big toe down with hydrogen peroxide. It had just been a nip. The rat hadn't broken skin. After a few minutes, I was on with police dispatch.

"Someone just threw a rat on my neighbor's lawn," I said.

"Threw a *what?*" said the dispatch woman.

"A rat. He stopped his car at my curb and threw a rat. I don't know if you want to call animal control or what?"

She assured me that the police would keep a look out for the offending car.

"You probably get weird calls like this all the time," I said.

"Not really," she said.

When I got off the phone, I stomped around the room a little.

"Why?" I said. "Why can't I ever go outside in my own neighborhood without something weird happening to me?"

"Why did you go outside without shoes on?" Regina said.

"It was an EMERGENCY!" I said.

"Yes, dear," she said.

"I hate this neighborhood," I said. "We have to move."

An Immigrant's Take

By Laila Lalami

Laila Lalami was born in Rabat and educated in Morocco, Britain and the United States. Her fiction has appeared in *Mizna*, *The Baltimore Review*, *First Intensity* and in the anthology *Arab Diaspora in Literature*. Her articles and essays have been published in *The Los Angeles Times*, *The Los Angeles Review*, *The Independent* and *The Nation*. Her debut book of fiction, *Hope and Other Dangerous Pursuits*, was published in October 2005. She is also the editor of the popular literary blog Moorishgirl.com. She lives in Portland, Oregon.

I remember clearly the first time I voted. It was on November 7, 2000, and I was 32 years old.

At the time, I was working for a software start-up company in Los Angeles. When I returned to my desk with an "I voted!" sticker on my shirt, one of my colleagues asked me if it was true that it was my first time voting. "Oh yes," I said. I hadn't bothered to vote in Morocco, where I was born and raised, because elections hadn't mattered. The results, under King Hassan's regime, were known in advance.

We had a pleasant chat, while leaning over our respective cubicle walls, about the current election in the States, about the process, and about what was at stake. We spent the rest of the day obsessively reloading online news sites and checking election results. When I went to bed that night, Fox News had called Florida for George W. Bush, but by next morning, there was still no president-elect.

I'd become an American citizen only four months before, at a ceremony held at a hangar in Pomona, California, on a day when temperatures reached 110 degrees. As I pledged to abjure fidelity to foreign potentates and swore allegiance to the United States, I felt overcome by the solemnity of the moment, by the sense of having changed the numbers on the ticket issued to me by the lottery of birth. In the summer of 2000, during the last days of the Clinton administration, there was a sense of optimism in the air: Unemployment was at four percent, there was a budget surplus, and the biggest worry among my friends seemed to be whether the NASDAQ would stay above 4,000.

I hadn't come to America with the huddled masses yearning to be free, but, more pragmatically, to attend graduate school. Along the way, I had seen a president have to answer for his actions before Congress, watched politicians debate the merits of their plans before the electorate, heard people agree and disagree, and the vibrancy of those exchanges had touched me profoundly. When I applied to become a U.S. citizen, it wasn't because I hated Morocco, my country of birth (quite the contrary), but because I loved America.

What I cherished most about America was the Bill of Rights—the guarantees that the Constitution provides for in the protection of individuals' rights—and the system of checks and balances—assurances that no single branch of government would overstep its powers.

It turned out that 2000 wasn't a bad year to start voting. It was a crash course on all things that make an election not just the biggest test of a democracy, but also its trickiest—invalid ballots, hanging chads, hand recounts, and so on.

Then came *Bush v. Gore*, and as I listened to the oral arguments on the radio on my way to work, I was surprised, confused and, above all, disappointed. I never thought that the Supreme Court would find time constraints to be more important than the rights of individuals to have their votes counted, that it would overrule the decisions of a state court in direct contradiction of the principles of federalism, and that it would essentially declare one of the candidates a victor.

This is what I signed up for? I thought. The idea of having a group of nine people decide the outcome of an election was too close for comfort for those who, like me, had once lived under authoritarian regimes. What gave me hope was that a working democracy is self-correcting, and so, despite having an appointed president, surely the United States would eventually find itself on the right track again.

Then came September 11th. Like so many others on the West Coast, I was woken by a ringing phone, in time to watch the second plane crash into the South Tower of the World Trade Center. Even today, more than four years later, words fail to describe the horror of that moment, the sight of people falling to their death, the plumes of smoke rising in the sky, the crumbling towers, the stampede of ash-covered survivors, the sound of their cries and screams recorded on live television. I knew there would be tough times ahead: for the survivors, for the victims' families, for the rescue workers, for all of us who had to learn to live in a new reality.

It was a time of great fear, and its concomitant emotion, hatred, was never too far. A couple of days after the attacks, I was pressing a coworker on a deadline and his response was, "What are you going to do? Shoot me? Isn't that how you people solve things?"

Forty-five days after the terrorist attacks, and with little debate or challenge, Congress passed the Patriot Act. Even in those confusing times, it was already clear what a setback it would be for civil liberties. The new law directly contradicted certain provisions of the Constitution. For instance, the FBI no longer had to show probable cause, as required by the Fourth Amendment, in order to access a person's financial, medical and library records. All it had to do was assert that the investigation was related to terrorism. The government could also prevent citizens who received search orders from telling others, thereby violating their First Amendment rights.

This is what I signed up for? I thought. I had valued the Bill of Rights above all other laws and now I had learned that it was not a constant, that the freedoms it guaranteed would be sacrificed for security. I thought of Benjamin Franklin. What gave me hope were the challenges mounted by liberals, activists and civil rights organizations like the ACLU. When hundreds of immigrants, all of them Middle-Eastern boys and men, were rounded up in 2003 in Southern California by Homeland Security under technicalities of a new registration order, the ACLU's efforts were instrumental in securing their ultimate release.

The Bush Administration's response to 9/11 strayed even further from this nation's ideals. The ever-changing rationale for the invasion of Iraq (weapons of mass destruction, removal of Saddam Hussein, saving the Kurds, making Iraq an example, bringing democracy to the Middle East, and so on) couldn't hide the plain truth: The war was a scam, the kind of thing one expects from nations run by dictators, not from the world's pre-eminent democracy. And yet, pointing out something like this only earned me the wrath of conservative friends. When I expressed my utter indignation over the torture at Abu-Ghraib, for instance, I was often told that it wasn't all that bad, "compared with what happens every day in those countries." With an eyebrow raised in my direction, the allusion was clear: Who was I to criticize the United States when I, of all people, should know what goes on in prisons throughout the Arab world?

This "love it or leave it" argument is not new, and it remains as foolish now as it was during the Vietnam War. War is ugly, and there aren't special exemptions for Americans. When a country sets out to free other people (people who have, as Joseph Conrad said, "[a] slightly darker complexion and slightly flatter noses") then it ought to behave in ways that uphold rather than desecrate the values it wants to spread. Besides, conservative critics have it the wrong way. It is *because* I am a new citizen that I am so upset about the turn the country has taken under Bush and the Republicans. Rather than cheering for the government, we ought to question it and hold it accountable for its actions.

These days, it seems that the only people willing to question are liberals. After all, it was a liberal—a veteran journalist—who dared to expose what was going on at Abu-Ghraib.

This is what I signed up for: a Supreme Court that upholds the Constitution, a Congress that does more than just rubber stamp new laws, and a president who respects international law. Under liberal rule in the 1990s, these were more than just ideals; they were guiding principles. There are many people working to restore these ideals: Justice Ruth Bader Ginsburg, who warned that the presidency of the United States should not be judged by whether or not a recount is "impractical;" Senator Barbara Boxer, who refused to follow the mad rush to war and voted against the joint resolution to invade Iraq; and the many, many liberals who are working for a change in leadership. These are things worth fighting for, and I believe liberals can regain them.

Media Matters: This Is Fair and Balanced

Wanted: Liberals to Revive Our Democracy

By Danny Schechter

News Dissector Danny Schechter is the "blogger-in-chief" of Mediachannel.org and director of the film *WMD* (Weapons of Mass Deception), about the media coverage of the war in Iraq. See www.wmdthefilm.com for more information.

I was practically born a liberal. My dad always voted on Line C for New York's Liberal Party. In college I belonged to the Cornell Liberal Union, a holdover from the 1950s when conservative versus liberal signaled a real distinction.

Back then, we all liked the *ideas* of liberalism: "free from bigotry, open to new ideas, tolerant, broad-minded," etc. Liberals supported government programs and civil rights and the good society. Our gurus were small-d democratic apostles like Arthur Schlesinger and New Deal economists like Ken Galbraith. We read magazines like Norman Cousins' *Saturday Review* and went all the way for Adlai Stevenson for President. When Tom Lehrer sang his satirical "love me, I am a liberal," we all sang along.

And then came Camelot. JFK wasn't really a liberal, but he played one on TV. However, his administration, with its Peace Corps and Alliance for Progress and civil-rightsy feel-good outlook seemed to show that liberalism could guide a nation.

Looking back, those were innocent times, uncontaminated by wars, cultural and otherwise, and the revolutionary rhetoric that rocked the 60s and moved the axis of ideological debate to the left.

In 1968, the Democratic Party imploded on the streets of Chicago as New Left activists and civil rights warriors battled the party regulars and the party's candidate, Vice-President Hubert Humphrey, who exemplified everything that was good and bad about liberals. To the kids, he was mealy-mouthed and compromising; to his backers, he represented the politics of the possible.

As a civil rights activist turned anti-war activist, I was in the first camp, and came to see the liberals as the enemy—spineless people who were selling us out. Richard Nixon and a generation of Republican rule were the beneficiaries of that perhaps unavoidable turmoil.

Ironically, even as liberals became discredited by the left, they were targeted as the source of all evil by the right, who, after many years in the political wilderness, saw liberalism as a powerful force that had to be dismantled.

As a result, even as they won electoral victories, and liberalism fused into pragmatism and opportunism, the right made fighting the "L-word" into an obsessive jihad. George Bush I saw "L" as a form of hell and ran against the ACLU. The GOP targeted "liberal" judges and "liberal" courts. They complained about "tax and spend liberals." Right-wing ideologists gussied up a campaign against the media and labeled it with a one-word smear: "liberalmediaelite."

However, as a media critic, I have yet to find that liberal media. In fact, like Gandhi famously said about Western civilization, it would be a "good idea." As Eric Alterman, who has written a book on the subject, notes, "the liberal media" is a "a myth, to be certain, but a useful one. If only it were true, we might have a more humane, open-minded, and ultimately effective public debate on the issues facing the nation. Alas, if pigs could fly. . ."

Our Republican Guard relies on Murdoch-owned media assets like the Fox News Channel, supportive newspapers, aggressive talk-radio hosts, conservative columnists and an arsenal of on-air pundits adept at polarizing opinion and devaluing independent journalism. They in turn benefit from a media environment shaped by a wave of media consolidation and the merger of news biz and showbiz. Entertainment-oriented reality shows help depoliticize viewers, while sensation-driven cable news limits analytical journalism and in-depth, issue-oriented coverage.

Is it any wonder then, that most Americans admit to being uninformed about many of the key issues we confront? Is it surprising that many blindly follow feel-good slogans or appeals to national unity and conformity? This media problem is at the heart of all the issues that we face. And it is not getting better.

Today, we live in two worlds of news and information. One is "fact-based," the other "faith-based." In the former, we cling to a world of objective reporting and verifiable evidence even as we know that the facts are skewed by media outlets with undisclosed agendas; in the latter, we only acknowledge facts that support our opinions and often don't let these facts get in the way of a "good argument." As the late Senator Patrick Daniel Moynihan put it, "Everyone is entitled to his own opinion, but not his own facts."

A good example of this is discerning the truth of the Iraq war. A prominent media critic with whom I was on a panel revealed that she recently interviewed many leading TV news anchors, and they could not agree on the causes of the war. "I was shocked by their lack of a consensus," she said. So, now we learn that while they all reported the war in the same way, many did not all believe what they were saying.

Another example: the 2004 election. At one point President Bush acknowledged that there was no connection between Osama bin Laden and Saddam Hussein and said that no WMDs were found in Iraq. Despite the fact that he said this, a majority of his supporters refused to change their long-held views, telling pollsters that they still believed the weapons were there, and that Iraq was linked to Al-Qaeda. The GOP campaign did nothing to correct this misperception.

Sadly, it will take a long time for truth to trickle out under the mounds of misinformation currently suffocating us. In my book *American Monsters*, I wrote about president William McKinley, who launched the Spanish American War with the slogan "Remember the Maine." Thanks to the yellow journalists of that era, Americans were convinced that the war was justified based on the "fact" that Spanish terrorists blew up our battleship in Havana Harbor. Fifty years later, we learned that the ship went down because of an accident in the engine room.

This same refusal to face the facts goes on every day. Incomplete stores, tilted accounts, distorted news. It's not just that some journalists today are on the government payroll. The rot in our corporate media goes deeper.

What can we believe? Who can we trust? What is true?

If we want to save our democracy, we have to press the media to do its constitutionally protected job as a watchdog on the people in power. We must insist that all views be given access, and that concerns of critics of this administration be heard and debated.

And, if we want a return to liberal values and a new, more relevant liberalism, we have to commit to a multicultural vision and to a campaign to inform the American people about the issues. That means we will have to challenge media trivialization and depoliticization. If a more robust liberalism is to play a more dynamic role in these turbulent times, we will need to find answers to the fundamental questions our media currently does not cover.

Crox News

By Jen Sorensen

Jen Sorensen is the cartoonist behind *Slowpoke*, a weekly strip which appears in magazines and alternative newspapers around the country. *Slowpoke* made its debut as a weekly strip in 1998, and has since won three awards from the Association of Alternative Newsweeklies, including First Place in 2005.

SLOWPOKE

© Jen Sorensen

www.slowpokecomics.com

Economics: Down with Trickle Down

Truly Liberal Democrace—Not "The Free Market"—Will Save America's Middle Class

by Thom Hartmann

Thom Hartmann is an award-winning, bestselling author, and the host of a nationally syndicated progressive daily radio talk show that is heard across America.

Here are a couple of headlines for those who haven't had the time to study both economics and history:

1. There is no such thing as a "free market."
2. The "middle class" is the creation of government intervention in the marketplace, and wouldn't exist without it (as millions of Americans and Europeans are discovering).

The conservative belief in "free markets" is a bit like the Catholic Church's insistence, in the 12th century, that the Earth was at the center of the solar system: It's widely believed by those in power, those who challenge it are branded heretics and ridiculed, and it is wrong. In fact, outside of local barter systems there is no such thing as a "free market." Markets larger than local barter systems are the creation of governments.

Governments provide a stable currency to make markets possible. They provide a legal infrastructure and court systems to enforce the contracts that make markets possible. They provide educated workforces through public education, and those workers show up at their places of business after traveling on public roads, rails or airways provided by government. Businesses that use "free markets" are protected by police and fire departments provided by government. They send their communications—from phone to fax to internet—over lines that follow public rights-of-way that are maintained and defended by government.

And, most important, the rules of the game of business are defined by government. Any sports fan can tell you that football, baseball or hockey without rules and referees would be a mess. Similarly, business without rules won't work.

Which explains why conservative economics wiped out the middle class during the period from 1880 to 1932, and why, when Reagan again began applying conservative economics, the middle class again began to vanish in America in the 1980s, a process that has dramatically picked up steam under both conservative Republicans and "conservative Democrats" like Bill Clinton (who pushed through NAFTA and GATT/WTO).

The conservative mantra is "let the market decide." But there is no market independent of government, so what they're really saying is, "Stop government from defending workers and building a middle class, and let the corporations decide how much to pay for labor and how to trade." This is, at best, destructive to national and international economies and, at worst, destructive to democracy itself.

Markets are a creation of government, just as corporations exist only by authorization of government. Governments set the rules of the market. And, since our government is of, by and for We The People, those rules have historically been set to maximize the public good resulting from people doing business. If you want to play the game of business, we've said in the U.S. since 1784 (when Tench Coxe got the first tariffs passed "to protect domestic industries"), then you have to play in a way that both makes you money *and* serves the public interest.

Which requires us to puncture the second balloon of popular belief: The "middle class" is not the natural result of freeing business to do whatever it wants, of "free and open markets" or of "free trade." The existence of a "middle class" is not the normal result of "free markets." In fact, it's the opposite—truly "free markets" will never produce a middle class. "Free markets" instead inevitably produce a small but powerful and wealthy ruling class, a very small "middle" mercantilist class, and a huge and terrified worker class (who in feudal times were called "serfs").

The middle class is a new invention of modern liberal democracies, the direct result of governments' intervening in and defining the rules of the game of business. It is, quite simply, an artifact of government regulation of markets and tax laws.

When government sets the rules of the game of business in such a way that working people must receive a living wage, that labor has the power to organize into unions, just as capital can organize into corporations, a middle class will emerge. When government gives up these functions, that same middle class vanishes, and we return to the Dickens-era "normal" form of "free market" conservative economics, in which the rich get richer while the working poor are kept in a constant state of fear and anxiety so that the cost of their labor will always be cheap.

The fact that the "marketplace" was an artifact of government activity was well-known to our founders. As Thomas Jefferson said in an 1803 letter to David Williams, "The greatest evils of populous society have ever appeared to me to spring from the vicious distribution of its members among the occupations . . . But when, by a blind concourse, particular occupations are ruinously overcharged and others left in want of hands, the national authorities can do much towards restoring the equilibrium."

And the "national authorities," in Jefferson's mind, should be the Congress, as he wrote in a series of answers to the French politician de Meusnier in 1786: "The commerce of the States cannot be regulated to the best advantage but by a single body, and no body so proper as Congress."

Of course, there were conservatives (like Hamilton and Adams) in Jefferson's time who, too, took exception, thinking that the trickle-down theory that had dominated feudal Europe for ten centuries was a stable and healthy form of governance. Jefferson took exception, in an 1809 letter to members of his Democratic Republican Party (now called the Democratic Party), saying: "The care of human life and happiness, and not their destruction, is the first and only legitimate object of good government."

But, conservatives say, government is the problem, not the solution. Of course, they can't explain how it was that the repeated series of huge tax cuts for the wealthy by the Hoover administration brought us the Great Depression, while raising taxes to provide for an active and interventionist government to protect the rights of labor to organize throughout the 1930s, 40s and 50s led to the Golden Age of the American Middle Class. (The top tax rate in 1930 under Hoover was 25 percent, and even that was only paid by about a fifth of wealthy Americans. Thirty years later, the top tax rate was 91 percent, and held at 70 percent until Reagan began dismantling the middle class. As the top rate dropped, so did the middle class it helped create.)

Jefferson pointed out in an 1816 letter to William H. Crawford that "every society has a right to fix the fundamental principles of its association." He also pointed out in that letter that some people—and businesses—would prefer that government not play referee to the game of business, not fix rules that protect labor or provide for the protection of the commons and the public good. We must, Jefferson wrote to Crawford, ". . . say to all [such] individuals, that if they contemplate pursuits beyond the limits of these principles and involving dangers which the society chooses to avoid, they must go somewhere else for their exercise; that we want no citizens, and still less ephemeral and pseudo-citizens [like corporations], on such terms. We may exclude them from our territory, as we do persons infected with disease."

Most of the founders advocated—and all ultimately passed—tariffs to protect domestic industries and workers. Seventy years later, Abraham Lincoln actively stood up for the right for labor to organize, intervening in several strikes to stop corporations and local governments from using hired goon squads to beat and murder strikers.

But conservative economics—the return of ancient feudalism—rose up after Lincoln's death and reigned through the Gilded Age, creating both great wealth and a huge population of what today we call the "working poor." American reaction to these disparities gave birth to the populist, progressive and modern labor movements. Two generations later, Franklin Roosevelt brought us out of Herbert Hoover's conservative-economics-produced Great Depression and bequeathed us with more than a half-century of prosperity.

But now the conservatives are back in the driver's seat and steering us back toward feudalism and serfdom (and possibly another Great Depression). Only a return to liberal economic policies—a return to We The People again setting and enforcing the rules of the game of business—will reverse this dangerous trend. We've done it before, with tariffs, anti-trust legislation and worker protections ranging from enforcing the rights of organized labor to restricting American companies' access to cheap foreign labor through visas and tariffs. The result was the production of something never before seen in history: a strong and vibrant middle class.

If the remnants of that modern middle class are to survive—and grow—we must learn the lessons of the past and return to the policies that in the 1780s and the late 1930s brought this nation back from the brink of economic disaster.

Intelligently Designed: Religion and Philosophy

Such Is the Human Race: A Pessimist's Defense of Liberalism and Fact-Based Public Education

By Maud Newton

Maud Newton is the proprietress of the popular literary and political

blog www.maudnewton.com

Proclaiming loyalty to my country wasn't enough at the fundamentalist elementary school I attended as a child. Every morning, after the pledge to the American flag, we also declared our allegiance to the Christian flag—white, with a red cross on a blue square in the top corner—and to the Bible. We promised to make "God's Holy Word" "a lamp unto my feet and a light unto my path," and to "hide its words in my heart, that I might not sin against God."

This rote devotional set the tone for the rest of the school day. Not only did we sit through a Bible class, where we read parables ("Earthly stories with a Heavenly meaning!") and were assigned verses to memorize, but spiritual instruction permeated every subject, bleeding even into history and science. There was no demarcation between faith and fact. What we learned of the world is neatly summarized in the first sentence of the first chapter of the first book of the Bible, Genesis 1:1. It reads, simply, "In the beginning God created the heavens and the earth." And the school was, and still is, upfront about its Evangelical mission. On its website, a letter from the principal to parents of prospective students begins: "The basic questions of life are effectively answered from the Scriptures, which are taught at King's Christian School."

Even as a child, I was troubled by the emphasis on blind faith, by the pressure to accept without question that God created the world in seven days and seven nights and sent His only Son to die and redeem us from our sins. My parents were fundamentalists, but they were converts. I remembered a life before religion, before the afternoon my parents came into my room, holding hands (a sure sign that something was amiss), filled me in on the high points of salvation, and instructed me to "accept Jesus into my heart." A few years after my mandatory conversion, my parents split ways in their religious convictions. Both continued to call themselves Christians, and both were, in the eyes of the rest of the world, still fundamentalists, but they argued, explosively, over the finer points of their respective catechisms. My mom took to speaking in tongues and casting out demons. My father remained attached to Presbyterianism, with its insistence that every aspect of our lives is charted out by God before we even appear in the world. In private, each of them tried to convince me that his or her view was the One True Way.

Pulled in both directions, and remembering a time before God was even an issue, I began to see religion as a personal—and somewhat relative—choice. I doubted the existence of God. And I started down a path of agnosticism that I've rarely strayed from since. But my education, through all of this, remained steadfastly Christ-centered. Apart from my father's old encyclopedias (which dated from the late '40s), I didn't have access to hard science or true history. I had only what I learned at school.

Public education was the antidote to all of this. I left the fundamentalist school at fourteen and entered ninth grade at a public junior high school. There I learned proper biology, secular world history, a smattering of the mythology I'd been forbidden to read. This being Miami, my classmates were more likely to be Jewish or Catholic than fundamentalist. But neither they nor my teachers ever mentioned God in the classroom, and as whole new worlds—ancient Babylonia, the Paleozoic era—opened up to me, I became convinced that keeping personal religious conviction separate from subjects like history and science meant better learning. My later education at a state university in Florida only reinforced this belief—one that most people outside my parents' orbit seemed then to take for granted.

Shortly before I moved from Florida to Brooklyn in 1999, Jeb Bush won the Florida gubernatorial election and managed to push through a school voucher program that allowed parents to send their kids to private religious schools with dollars that would otherwise go into public education's coffers. My friends and I were stunned by this blurring of the line between church and state. And unlike most of my friends, I'd experienced firsthand the ways disinformation is peddled in private religious schools. I couldn't believe state dollars were going to subsidize such blatantly lopsided instruction.

Fast-forward seven years, and my surprise at state vouchers paying for faith-based instruction starts to seem quaintly naïve. Parents in public school districts from Georgia and Texas to Pennsylvania have begun to demand that "intelligent design" (a fancy, scientific-sounding name for creationism) be given equal weight with evolution in the science curriculum. It's a matter of fairness, they say. And last year Cobb County, Georgia, placed evolution warning stickers on textbooks: "Evolution is a theory, not a fact, regarding the origin of living things." The media covered the story, but with that look-at-what-those-funny-people-in-the-South-are-up-to-now tone that completely misses the point. Ultimately a judge ordered the stickers removed, but similar cases—involving the teaching of intelligent design, rather than warning stickers—are springing up around the country.

In 1987, the Supreme Court ruled unconstitutional the

teaching of creationism as science in public schools, but the make-up of the court has changed drastically since then. One justice, Clarence Thomas, has argued in dissenting opinions that the U.S. Constitution would allow states to create official churches. Whether Bush's new appointees will agree is anyone's guess. But even if the court doesn't overtly repudiate its prior holding, advocates of "intelligent design" are trying to pave the way for deviation from precedent by arguing, in essence, and bewilderingly, that their faith-based theory amounts to science rather than creationism because neither the Bible nor God is ever mentioned. Under that reasoning, "science" becomes a word empty of meaning, a sort of creationist Affirmative Action program—and ironically, one supported by the same people who otherwise oppose fairness in education—in which belief is given equal weight with tested and proven (at least, until disproved) hypotheses.

Admittedly, the public schools have never been entirely free from religion, Supreme Court ruling or no. A Catholic friend of mine grew up in a small Central Florida town where fundamentalist prayers, ending with something like an altar call, opened her public school day. But presumably the textbooks were standardized, even if the "moment of silence" wasn't.

Common sense suggests that even if 51 percent of the country supported a second Bush term, the majority of Americans probably do not favor scientifically inaccurate textbooks for their children—particularly not scientifically inaccurate textbooks purchased with their own tax dollars. Unfortunately, if recent polls are to be believed, common sense is not borne out in this case. A clear majority of poll respondents say they believe that "intelligent design" should be given equal weight with evolution in science textbooks.

As Mark Twain famously said, "Such is the human race. Often it does seem such a pity that Noah and his party did not miss the boat." But miss the boat, according to the Bible, they did not. And if intelligent design makes it into our science books, how long before alternate versions of history must be offered as well? I can just see it now: Noah's flood presented as civilization's starting-point; Moses and the burning bush taught alongside Egyptian history; Christ's suffering, death and resurrection given equal weight with what we know of ancient Rome.

I identify as a liberal (to the extent that I identify as a member of any political group), not because I have some pie-in-the-sky belief in the fundamental goodness of humankind, but because I do not. Winston Churchill said of majority rule: "No one pretends that democracy is perfect or all-wise. Indeed, it has been said that democracy is the worst form of Government except all those others that have been tried." He also said: "The best argument against democracy is a five-minute conversation with the average voter."

A majority, left unchecked, can trample the rights of individual citizens. The founders of our country realized this danger. And to protect individuals and members of minority groups from the tyranny of the majority, they enacted ten amendments to the Constitution to ensure certain basic rights, including the right to worship freely (or not) whomever or whatever we may choose. This right, it now seems necessary to remind people, is plain on the face of the First Amendment, which guarantees "Freedom of speech, press, religion, peaceable assembly, and to petition the government. Congress shall make no law respecting an establishment of religion, or prohibiting the free exercise thereof."

Conservatives increasingly argue that the states can do what Congress can't, and perhaps they'll emerge triumphant. It is not inconceivable that, within our lifetimes, public schoolchildren in some states will be studying Genesis in science class, just as I once did. Yet one wonders how soon religious conservatives would change their tune about teaching creationism in the classroom if demographics shifted and the majority's religious impulses changed.

The bottom line is this: If I believed our planet and everyone on it were created by Marvin the Martian, well, bully for me. But my conviction, however sincere, should not be dressed up as science and imposed on other people. Parents have ample opportunity to indoctrinate their children on nights and weekends. State-sponsored science education should be just that: education, in science.

The Creed of a Liberal

By Ralph Temple

Ralph Temple served as legal director of the American Civil Liberties Union of the National Capital Area from 1966 to 1980, taught at the law schools of Harvard University (1958–59), George Washington University (1959–62), Howard University (1969–70) and Georgetown University (1975), and practiced law in Washington, DC, for forty years. He now lives and writes in Ashland, Oregon, where he is active with the Oregon ACLU.

The Three Core Beliefs of Liberals

Three basic beliefs define the American liberal, and are inherent in the liberal position on any issue: (1) that the collective society guarantees every individual the right to safety and the right to work, subsistence, education and health care; (2) that the individual does not exist for the protection of the state—to the contrary, the state exists for the protection of individual liberty; and (3) that some individual rights are so intrinsic that they may not be abridged, even if the majority of the people do not agree.

The seeds of the first principle appear in the opening lines of the Constitution:

"We the People of the United States, in Order to form a more perfect Union, establish Justice, insure domestic Tranquillity, provide for the common defense, promote the general Welfare, and secure the Blessings of Liberty to ourselves and our Posterity, do ordain and establish this Constitution for the United States of America."[1]

The second principle is fundamental to the concept of America. It was the very purpose of our constitutional system and the Bill of Rights to establish a form of government in which the autonomy and integrity of the individual would predominate over the interests of the state, the collective society—the public. The philosophy is that the primary purpose of the state is the preservation and advancement of individual liberty, compromised only to the extent indispensable to safety and welfare.

The third principle is found in the opening lines of the Declaration of Independence:

"We hold these truths to be self-evident, that all men are created equal, that they are endowed by their Creator with certain unalienable rights, that among these are Life, Liberty and the pursuit of Happiness." [2]

You don't have to believe in God to appreciate that the phrase "endowed by their Creator" means that some rights are so basic, so axiomatic, that they are inherent in the human condition, and that no person, group or cause can justify their abridgment. This belief is inherent to the liberal creed.

In sum, the liberal's core beliefs are essentially American, deeply embedded in our country's founding philosophy and character. To be a liberal is to be committed to what makes America unique in history and in the world.

These three beliefs contain two fundamental and complex challenges: first, where to draw the line between safety and the public welfare on the one hand, and individual liberty on the other; and, second—a broader restatement of the first—how to reconcile the paradoxes presented by liberty and order.

John Rawls's Theory of Justice

The first of these, the challenge of how to conceptualize the just allocation of power between the community and the individual, was taken on by philosopher John Rawls in his 1971 classic, *A Theory of Justice*.[3] Rawls asked us to imagine a group of people voting on what the distribution of power should be, between the individual and the collective society, but doing so under a "Veil of Ignorance," that is, without knowing where each of them would be in the power structure once the rules went into effect.

What kind of individual rights against the whole society would you vote for if you didn't know when you woke up tomorrow whether you would be black or white, Arab, Christian, Jewish or Muslim, rich or poor, in the racial, ethnic, religious or political majority or minority, and so forth? Under the "Veil of Ignorance," Rawls theorized, each person, having to decide on the rights each of them would have, and what steps the collective group might take against each of them, would be forced by self-interest to balance his or her personal desire for law and order—that is, harmony and protection from crime—against the desire for certain rights in case he or she became the target of group sentiment or action.

Rawls concluded that when people are compelled to put themselves in another person's place and to choose laws that treat others the way they themselves would want to be treated if they were on the receiving end of societal disfavor, the chances are they will end up where the founders did, with a set of individual rights approximating those in the Bill of Rights of the United States Constitution.

Similarly, applying the Rawls theory of justice to an economic system, people operating under a veil of ignorance, without knowing if they'll end up in a society in which their skills will succeed or fail, would have to balance their desire for prosperity and wealth against the need for protection against potential poverty. Reasonable people making such decisions would probably vote for an economic system that allowed wealth and luxury but capped them off with taxes at a level sufficient to provide a social safety net for those who, inevitably in every society, end up on the bottom.

Liberals Accept Life's Challenge of Paradox

The second challenge of liberal beliefs comes from the paradox of reconciling liberty and order, a paradox inherent in life itself.

Liberals pursue fairness, justice, equality for all, and the maximum feasible individual liberty. But equality, an essential element of fairness and justice, is incompatible with liberty. If everyone is completely free, the strong will prosper and the weak will suffer. British economist and philosopher E. F. Schumacher noted that it was brilliant of the French, in their revolutionary slogan, to place between the opposites of "Liberty" and "Equality" the human virtue that reconciles them, "Fraternity," that is, brotherhood.[4]

So to be a liberal, one must be able to live and cope with paradox, one must embrace "fraternity," the oneness of all people. To be a liberal is to strive to master the essential ironies of life. The most universal and fundamental of life's paradoxes are life versus death, growth versus decay, change versus stability. From these come the great social and political paradox of liberty versus order that underlies the choices in all social structures.[5] It is a major virtue of the liberal that she struggles with this paradox rather than opting for one-sided resolutions that sacrifice one or the other.

A dramatic example of the liberal coping with this paradox is the American Civil Liberties Union's unwavering defense of freedom of speech, even for American Nazis and the Ku Klux Klan. Intrepid scholarly efforts have shown that it is impossible to construct a law that would ban the speech of these loathsome groups without undermining the free speech protections of all other dissident groups.[6] For if the government is given the power to suppress anyone's speech, no one's right of free speech is safe.

Coming to grips with this paradox also explains why liberals who are fervent in their faith, including priests and rabbis, nevertheless fight to keep religion out of the public schools. Ask a Christian fundamentalist if he wants prayer in the public schools if he is living in a Muslim-majority town and the prayer is likely to be addressed to Allah while facing Mecca.

The paradox came home to me in 1978 at the Jewish Community Center in Cleveland, where I was defending the ACLU's representation of the Nazis. It was a bitter pill to be confronted by Holocaust survivors in the audience while, outside, teenage Jewish pickets carried signs saying "Jews Who Defend Nazis Are an Abomination."[7]

Despite the unpopularity of the ACLU's position with the public, these cases are never hard ones for the courts, which see quite clearly the nature of the problem and invariably rule in favor of the free-speech rights of the Nazis and Klan. But the ACLU pays dearly for its stance. In 1978, the organization lost a quarter of its membership and funding when it fought for and won the right of the Nazis to march in Skokie, Illinois.

The Golden Rule

There is an ancient moral law that articulates the necessity of identifying with the other in dealing with life's paradoxes.[8] That law is the most profound virtue of liberalism, the transcendent tenet from which the three core liberal beliefs derive: the golden rule—"Do unto others as you would have others do unto you." Liberals believe that the Golden Rule should be the dominant social, political and economic doctrine of any society, and it is the principle at the foundation of Rawls' *A Theory of Justice*. This powerful canon is not exclusive to or even original with Christians, but it is universal and ageless and found, in nearly identical language, in almost all traditions, e.g., to name just a dozen:

Jewish (Hillel, 50 BC), Greek (Isocrates, 335 BC), Plato and Aristotle (fourth century BC), Thales (fifth century BC), Confucius (500 BC), Pittacus (650 BC), Hindu (the Mahabharata, 1000 BC) and Muslim, Buddhist, Roman, Persian and Native American.[9]

It is ironic that conservatives in general and the Christian right in particular claim the moral high ground, when so often their political, social and economic positions are the antitheses of this universal gospel. Liberals believe that what it takes to make the right cut between the collective good on the one hand and individual political and economic freedom on the other is kinship with all—the golden rule. That concept is at the heart of liberalism.

Notes

1. Preamble, U.S. Constitution
2. Thomas Jefferson, The Declaration of Independence, July 1776.
3. Harvard University Press, 1971.
4. E. F. Schumacher, *A Guide for the Perplexed* (Harper & Row, New York, 1977), at 12
5. Schumacher at 125
6. See, e.g., Monroe Freedman & Eric Freedman, *Group Defamation and Freedom of Speech* (Greenwood, 1995).
7. See *The Cleveland Plain Dealer*, February 17, 1978, D-2.
8. See, e.g., Martin Buber, *I and Thou* (1923)
9. See World Scripture at http://www.unification.net/ws/theme015.htm

A New Deal: Where We Go From Here

I'm a Big Fat Liberal

By Will Durst

A Midwestern baby boomer with a media-induced identity crisis, Will Durst has been called "a modern-day Will Rogers" by the *L.A. Times*, while the *S.F. Chronicle* hailed him as "heir apparent to Mort Sahl and Dick Gregory." This five-time Emmy nominee and host/co-producer of the ongoing award-winning PBS series "Livelyhood" is also a regular commentator on NPR and CNN, and has appeared on every comedy show featuring a brick wall including Letterman, Comedy Central, HBO and Showtime, receiving seven consecutive nominations for the American Comedy Awards Stand Up of the Year.

All right, let's not pussyfoot around here. I'll come right out and admit it: I'm a big fat liberal. Yes, that's right. A liberal. Not a Democrat. Not a libertarian. Not a moderate. Not a Greenie. Not a Naderite. Not whatever those people who vote for John Breaux and Lincoln Chafee are. Not a fiscal conservative. Not a social liberal. Not a dynamic forward thinker, or a person who leans left. Not a new liberal or a neo-liberal or a nouveaux liberal. Not a secularist or a pragmatist. Or a progressive. (Okay, maybe a progressive.) Not a small-l liberal. I'm a commie-pinko-yellow-rat-bastard-without-the-commie-part-big-fat-Liberal-with-a-capital-L.

I am who I am because of my background: a third-generation factory rat from Milwaukee, Wisconsin, whose father was let go six months before retirement so they didn't have to give him his full pension. I was taught that a society is judged on how it treats its least fortunate. And yes, I believe we should help them, *even if they don't want our help or refuse to do anything in return.* And yes, I think the most fortunate should be responsible for paying for it. And not only do I think they should ante up, I think they should be gosh-darn happy about it too. I want them to quit shirking their responsibility for their fortunate status in this country and see them smile while paying through the nose.

And, as a big fat liberal, I don't want to hear any more carping from the rich and the big corporations about how they're being bled to death by huge taxes. Total BS. They don't pay squat. Like the rest of us, they're lucky that they get to live in this country. Lucky our laws protect them. Lucky our leaders allow them to them rip us off through protected markets and ridiculous surcharges and exorbitant convenience fees. They're lucky they're free to pillage the populace here while hiding their obscene offshore profits. They're lucky they aren't dragged from their beds for sins against humanity and forced to spend the rest of their lives eating wet dirt behind razor wire patrolled by dogs and very large tattooed men with automatic weapons.

And, as a big fat liberal, I also want the rich to quit lying. To quit seducing the middle class with Lotto fantasies of all of us having a shot to make it big. I want them to quit filling the media with stories about the dignity of the poor. There is no dignity to being poor—just struggle. I want the rich to be fined every time they lie about democracy. Every time they get their lackeys to tell us that the rich getting richer is good for democracy. Every time they get their lackeys to tell us that torturing prisoners is good for democracy. Every time they get their lackeys to tell us that the death of innocent civilians is unfortunate collateral damage but necessary for democracy to work.

And, as a big fat liberal, I'm tired. Tired of oil companies posting monster profits and still whining about their lack of control over gas prices. Tired of a president who can't button his own shirt or ride a bike without falling over. Tired of Dick Cheney's evil smirk. Tired of being part of the only industrialized nation in the world without universal health care. Tired of Senator Doctor Indian Chief Bill Frist's smug condescension. Tired of being told I'm no good because God loves others more than me. Tired of being pitted against each other when we're all in this together.

I'm also tired of being afraid. So afraid that before I fly I'm forced to take off my shoes and worry about clean underwear and am prohibited from carrying nail clippers or a cigarette lighter on my person. Afraid I'm going to punch the next person in the nose who tells me that speaking out against our government's policy endangers our troops. Afraid the little clicking noises on my telephone mean I've just been designated a terrorist by Patriot Act II. Afraid of mysterious bogeymen who hate us for our freedoms, when it's obvious they hate us because we're bombing them into being more like us. And they don't want to be.

Besides, look around. This country is falling apart. The rich may not want to pay for the same services as the rest of us, but they use them just the same. The same fire departments. The same roads. The same emergency rooms. The same cops. (More cops, actually.) The same libraries. The same bridges. The same levees. (Admittedly, their houses are farther away.) The same schools. Okay, different schools. The same paramedics. The same garbage pickups. (Actually, much larger garbage pickups.) The same freeway exit ramps. The same Treasury Department, albeit with much greater access to the primary distribution product. The same harbor tugs. The same public transportation systems. Okay, they don't use public transportation, but since some of us do, it makes their commutes more reasonable.

It's never the liberals who want to get rid of regulations on pollution. It's never the liberals who want to abolish workers' rights. It's never the liberals who want to classify ketchup as a vegetable. It's never the liberals who want to cut winter-heating subsidies to the elderly so rich people can have more money. It's never the liberals who want to allow more logging in our national forests and drilling off our shores and the dumping of toxic wastes in our backyards. It's never the liberals who want to eliminate hot school lunches for underprivileged children and prenatal care and equal rights to all our citizens. Liberals are for all of these, not to mention puppies and sunshine and balloons.

If you look up the word "liberal" in the dictionary, the definition right after "free from bigotry" says "open to new ideas for progress, and tolerant of the ideas and behavior of others." Which is the whole problem. Tolerance. Our willingness to listen to others—including each other. And listen. And listen. And listen. We will eat our own, because our only currency is the truth. Which cannot be compromised.

But this country has seen enough of compassionate conservatism. This country has seen enough of preemptive gouging. This country has a severe case of Bush Fatigue and all that entails. Everyone who rose with him will fall with him. The pendulum is swinging back. We must grab the standard and run with it. There are people counting on us.

Patriotic Liberals Enlist in the War of Ideas

By Mark Green

Mark Green is president of the New Democracy Project. He's the former consumer affairs commissioner (1990–1993) and the elected public advocate of New York City (1994–2001), as well as the author or editor of nineteen books on public affairs.

There has been a gross disparity of resources in ideological clashes, certainly since Richard Mellon Scaife began investing hundreds of millions of dollars in conservative think tanks in the 1960s. The result: Large marble buildings in Washington house the American Enterprise Institute, the Heritage Foundation, the CATO Institute and dozens of others that often prevail in public opinion due more to volume than quality—although the gap started to shrink with the founding of the very substantial Center for American Progress in 2004.

These intensity and resource gaps are occurring at a transformational moment in both world and domestic affairs. In the past fifteen years, a historical blink of an eye really, the world has evolved from one dominated by an East-West superpowers' conflict to one with a sole hyper-power and many terrorist lilliputians—and from nation-based industrial economies to a more globalized information economy with far greater trade in goods and services.

Domestically, President Bush is pushing hard-right policies to excite his base and dominate politics and policies for decades. Sociologist Daniel Bell may have talked about "the end of ideology" in the 1950s, but Karl Rove and Tom DeLay weren't listening. After interviewing Rove at length and hearing him muse about a "period of dominance," *The New Yorker*'s Nicholas Lemann concluded that the man called "Bush's brain" had the goal of "creating a Republican majority that . . . would last for a generation and would wind up profoundly changing the relationship between citizen and state in this country." DeLay told a group of GOP activists, "For the first time in more than a century, the Republican Party is in the position to reshape American politics, and, therefore, reshape American society for more than a generation." Turning a deterministic Marx on his head, DeLay—before an indictment forced him from office—went on to boldly conclude that "instead of actions being dictated by the terms of history, the terms of history will be dictated by our actions."

Since "nothing succeeds like excess," the conservative movement now openly seeks the complete takeover of American politics. Johnson's crushing defeat of Goldwater—and 1965 legislative successes—seemed to presage an era of liberal dominance. Except that conservatives then rethought, reorganized, returned to the grassroots—and four years later won the presidency and sixteen years later the federal government as well. After Reagan's election in 1980, a jubilant William Rusher, publisher of the *National Review*, triumphantly announced, "Liberalism is dead." Triumphantly and prematurely, of course, since a center-left Democrat named Bill Clinton won the presidency a decade later. Twice.

To confuse matters more, there's much evidence that the country, in Lloyd Free and Hadley Cantril's useful dichotomy, is more than ever ideologically conservative but operationally liberal. There's a majority against "big government" *and* a majority for regulation to stop Enron and mad cow disease and to make sure that FEMA helps New Orleans survive rather than drown after a foreseeable disaster—a majority for "lower taxes" *and* a majority for spending more on environmental safety.

Indeed, on issue after issue, with the sole exception of national security—from education, health care and jobs to the environment, consumer justice and reproductive rights—the country sides with liberal policies more than conservative ones. There is then a large policy gap that liberals could exploit if they developed a competing, compelling narrative to the prevailing one focusing on taxes and terrorism.

Real patriots who love an ever-improving America should now ask whether a policy or program advances the middle class, collective security, a stronger democracy—and One America. For a quarter century of conservative doctrine from Reagan to Bush has inflicted great harm on average families and global problem solving. Is it patriotic to say that you love your country but hate your government? To cut taxes for the super-rich during wartime while asking soldiers to risk their lives? Public policy from now on should focus on how to build a stronger America on four basic cornerstones:

Strengthen the Middle Class. There has been an historic, largely unheralded redistribution of wealth in the past three decades from the stretched middle class to the already wealthy. It began with the incipient globalization and oil shocks of the 1970s and continued with the climbing stock market in the 1990s. It accelerated, however, as George Bush redistributed wealth more than George McGovern was ever accused of—except upward rather than downward. His tax cuts—on income, estates, dividends, capital gains, corporate earnings—was a program of plutocracy posing as populism. While the public rationale was economic growth and the rhetoric was "it's your money," in effect nearly half of "our" money somehow flowed to the top 1 percent of all income earners.

At what point will "NASCAR dads" or "Reagan Democrats" realize that Republicans who campaign on guns and gays and God seek to distract them from the reality that they're working harder, earning less and tolerating a world in which their children will be economically worse off? One explanation is that more people in blind taste tests say they *like* Pepsi, yet more people *buy* Coke—it's the psychological triumph of branding. A party of flags and faith has proven, recently, to be a politically superior brand.

It's time to become liberal hawks in the class war of ideas. Instead of simply being reactivists—a little more tax equity, please—it's time for a new narrative other than plutocracy at home and preemption abroad. For the ideological debate in America today is less left-right and more up-down. The Party of CEOs versus the Party for Children—a trillion more for the top 1 percent or a trillion more for school construction, teacher recruitment and smaller classes. Why is it called class warfare to want to go back to the tax rates of Ronald Reagan? And if the conservatives' trump card is economic growth rather than "tax-and-spend liberalism," how do they respond to the fact that from FDR to W, the average GDP under Republican presidents has been 2.8 percent, while under Democratic presidents, 5.1 percent?

Public policy, consequently, should constantly attempt to protect the middle class from slipping into poverty and help those in poverty enter the middle class. We need specific ways to strengthen the struggling middle-class, from creating a living wage, making health care more affordable, providing for pre-K and after-school programs, shrinking class size, K-3, and investing in job training rather than nation-building—paid for by shrinking corporate welfare and reversing the overgenerous and unproductive tax cuts for the top 2 percent.

Strengthen Collective Security. When President Bush said to great applause in his 2004 State of the Union Address that

Patriotic Liberals Enlist in the War of Ideas

"America will never seek a permission slip to defend the security of our country," it was a near perfect example of Bill Clinton's adage that Americans prefer someone who is strong and wrong to someone who appears weak and right. At the level of rhetorical sound bite, the "permission slip" reference is a big winner. Of course America has not and will not cede its destiny to others. But at the same time, government officials had better understand the admonition of Michael Tomasky, executive editor of the *American Prospect.* "America is not an empire, it is a democracy. A democracy leads the world but it does not seek to rule it."

In this context, the perception of America as the Lone Ranger and allies as an unquestioning Tonto is hopelessly counterproductive. Simply walking away from the ABM Treaty, Kyoto Protocol, Small Arms Agreement, International Criminal Court, Chemical and Biological Weapons Convention and U.N. Commission on the Status of Women—as well as our bungle in Iraq—has soured the populations of nearly every nation in the world and isolated America.

Just as wealthy families realized that communal fire and police departments were preferable to private militia in the 1800s, collective security makes us stronger, not weaker. "The most important reason for the United States to commit itself to rules," wrote Anne-Marie Slaughter, dean of the Woodrow Wilson School of Public and International Affairs at Princeton University, "is not because they will restrain our enemies but because they will reassure our friends—and without our friends we cannot in the end defeat our enemies."

Strengthen Democracy. One of the prevailing ironies of political life is how some American warriors are eager to cross oceans to fight for democracy but uninterested—or even opposed—to expanding it at home. Over two centuries, it was wealthy elites, open racists and flag-draped "patriots" who pushed for property, racial, gender, literacy and registration barriers to voting. This is a current struggle, as measured by the contradiction between our July 4th rhetoric about freedom and democracy and the reality that, of the 22 Western democracies, only Botswana has a lower turnout of eligible adults voting. While European allies such as Great Britain, France and Germany regularly have 70 percent-plus majorities voting, only a third of eligible Americans vote in congressional elections.

We need to update Jefferson's insight that America should stand for "equal rights for all, special privileges for none." For if the laws governing voting and contributing mean that those who govern us respond more to donors than voters, then there's little prospect of enacting needed consumer, environmental, housing and education laws.

One America. In Ric Burns's *New York*, the narrator describes our largest city in words that characterize our country as well. New York is "a continuing experiment to see if all the peoples of the world can live together in one small space." While America is of course a place divided into numerous ethnicities, races, religions and cultures, all proud of their history and heritage, each group should not live in their separate silos from where they look on others as threatening or unworthy. We are, after all, the *United* States of America.

Yet when we began the 20th century, the great black scholar W.E.B. DuBois predicted that the new centennial, coming only 35 years after the Civil War, would be dominated by "the color line." He was right. But will it dominate not only the 19th and the 20th centuries but the 21st as well?

Race has been far less discussed in recent years in part

because different racial constituencies are on such political hair-triggers that few politicians think it worth the risk of offending someone—or everyone. It's nonetheless urgent that we acknowledge—and try to bridge—our racial divides. Can we really afford to continue to have two-thirds of black children born out –of wedlock? Latino families' net worth averaging one-twenty-fifth of that of white families? An unemployment rate of 50 percent for African-American men ages 16-64 in New York City?

We must more resolutely stand for equality and justice, because equal opportunity remains an unfulfilled promise for too many Americans merely due to their race, religion, national origin or sexual orientation. But how can a president and Congress accomplish this in an era where discrimination comes not in the form of hooded vigilantes but politicians in dark suits and big smiles arguing against "reverse discrimination" and "special rights"?

Four options come to mind. We need more candidates and officeholders who can comfortably speak to and for white, black, Hispanic *and* Asian audiences, as Robert Kennedy did so well in the mid-1960s—and Bill Clinton 30 years later. We need other politicians to stop exploiting racial tensions by new versions of Nixon's "southern strategy." We need to face race and not act as if indifference is a solution. Last, we should look more to universal solutions based on need rather than complexion in order to mobilize majority coalitions. Better health care, public transit, public schools and environmental regulation can simultaneously be more readily enacted and disproportionately help minorities enduring poorer schools, no health insurance and dirty air. White and non-white politicians, therefore, should complete an anti-discrimination agenda, but also go further to enact an "opportunity agenda," which in turn would require that we transcend race in order to include all in the promise of America.

In 1808 Thomas Jefferson drew up plans to develop the West, and we did. In 1908, Theodore Roosevelt conceived of how to preserve our natural resources, and our national parks and environmental movements were born. In the 1930s, FDR created a latticework of regulatory agencies that "saved capitalism from itself" and provided a safety net for people in need. Eisenhower constructed an interstate highway system that economically proved to be the Erie Canal of the 20th century. By "throwing his hat over the wall of space," Kennedy's Apollo program forever altered the way we think of ourselves and opened possibilities as yet unrealized. And more recently, civil rights laws, consumer laws, environmental laws, the Freedom of Information Act, the Americans with Disabilities Act, the Earned Income Tax Credit, and Family and Medical Leave Act proved to be breakthroughs that made America more prosperous and just. What's the next big or small idea or ideas that by 2010 could similarly change America?

At today's transformational moment, there *is* a clear, confident and credible set of policies that would work to truly change and strengthen our nation. These policies build on, but don't merely rely on, earlier generations of progressive programs.

1. Recommit to a new *global bargain for collective security* whereby the United States agrees to accept some constraints on its ability to use force in return for a genuine commitment by the nations of the world to do everything possible to combat terrorism, radical (armed) fundamentalism, the threat of failed states and nuclear proliferation.

2. *Transform America's military forces* and intelligence ser-

vices away from unilateralism and preemptive invasion and toward more human intelligence and swifter troop deployments.

3. Stop investing in an empire abroad and start *publicly investing in our economy* at home by such new approaches as a Federal Infrastructure Bank, Office of Capital Investment, and Revenue Sharing to states with sustained high unemployment so they don't cut services just when they're needed.

4. *End the tax cuts* for the top 2 percent and *reinvest the savings* into deficit reduction and health care.

5. *Save Social Security* by gradually increasing the ceiling on the amount of earnings subject to the payroll tax and gradually reducing benefits to those with very high lifetime earnings.

6. Embrace an urban-suburban *metropolitan agenda* that promotes smart growth, stimulates investment in metropolitan regions and connects low-income families to new employment and educational opportunities.

7. Toss out the unworkable No Child Left Behind law to focus not only on testing but also on *school construction, teacher recruitment and smaller class sizes* in earlier grades.

8. Base *health insurance on need,* not family status, and redraft the Medicare prescription drug benefit to allow more drug price competition to keep costs down and to increase coverage.

9. Adopt an *energy independence strategy* beginning with a 50 percent increase in auto fuel-efficiency standards over the next decade—and enforce environmental laws, again.

10. Pursue a *democracy agenda* that includes a) the public

financing of congressional elections, b) restrictions on self-financing (reversing *Buckley*), c) paper trails for electronic voting, d) elimination of discriminatory felony disenfranchisement laws, e) restrictions on further media concentration—and merging Veterans Day into a Democracy Day holiday the first Tuesday every November, when we pay respect to veterans who defended democracy by voting.

This agenda rejects messianic incompetence abroad and greed-is-good economics at home. It assumes that what matters is not bigger or smaller, but smarter, government, relentlessly progressing to restrict corporate power, to encourage entrepreneurs, to expand health care, to put inspiring teachers in front of small classes, to clean up the environment. That's a narrative in step with Walt Whitman's description of an America that's "always becoming." And that's a program for liberal patriotism worthy of our history and our future.

The Era of Big Government

By Matthew Yglesias

Matthew Yglesias is a staff writer at *The American Prospect*. His work has also appeared in *The New York Times Magazine*, the Center for American Progress website, and *Tech Central Station*. In addition, he appears frequently on radio shows (and, tragically, less frequently on television) throughout the nation. His blog can be found at http://yglesias.typepad.com

There are two things you need to know about American politics. One is that self-described conservatives outnumber self-described moderates by about a 3:2 margin and have done so for decades. The other is that during Ronald Reagan's first inaugural address, he said, "Government is not the solution to our problems—government is the problem." George W. Bush, however, has expounded the view that government should step in "wherever people are hurting."

The stasis surrounding what labels people place on their own political beliefs suggests that virtually nothing changes in American politics. The facts on the ground say otherwise. "Liberal" and "conservative" are just words—important words, to be sure—but they derive their importance from what people mean by them. In a 1953 interview with *The Saturday Evening Post*, John F. Kennedy said, "I'd be very happy to tell them I'm not a liberal at all." At the time, "liberal" was understood to denote a certain approach to the Cold War and strong support for civil rights.

In 2006, of course, the first issue has vanished entirely, while the most hardened conservative would proclaim himself an enthusiastic proponent of the view that black people should be allowed to vote and that everyone should drink from the same water fountain. At the same time, even a clear liberal like Adlai Stevenson had nothing in particular to say about abortion rights, now a high-profile liberal cause.

Until the passage of the Elementary and Secondary Education Act in 1965, the federal government did essentially nothing to finance American public education or subsidize poorer school districts. The view that it should do something in that area counted, at the time, as a liberal one. Eventually, it became a mainstream view. The Gingrich congress of the mid-1990s promised to eliminate the Department of Education, but even those "revolutionaries" did not actually propose to move the country back to the situation that had existed during Kennedy's term in office. Nowadays, of course, that plank is gone from the Republican platform, and George W. Bush has sponsored large increases in the department's budget and area of responsibilities.

Liberals, in other words, are a self-conscious avant-garde, destined, in a sense, to be a perpetual minority. But *liberalism* is a set of substantive policy commitments. Liberalism succeeds not by recruiting more self-described "liberals" but by sufficiently entrenching its ideas in the public imagination to the point where one no longer needs to be a liberal to support them. As a result, the fortunes of liberalism the word and liberalism the doctrine can diverge substantially. The word is no more popular in 2006 than it was in 1981, and liberals hold fewer of the levers of power today than we did back then, which can easily lead to the conclusion that things are bleaker than ever. But listen to what Bush is *saying* and a rather different picture forms.

We hear no Reaganesque promises from him to get the monkey of big government off our backs. Instead, we hear tell of a president whose fondest hope is to use the federal government to unleash "armies of compassion" upon the country to fight the scourges of drug addiction and poverty. A president who wants to beat the "soft bigotry of low expectations" and close the racial gap in educational achievement. A president who delivered a prescription drug benefit to the nation's senior citizens, and one whose administration is dedicated to promoting "clean skies" and "healthy forests."

Some observers have interpreted Bush's liberal rhetoric as a reaction to Hurricane Katrina, but in reality it's been there from the beginning. In recent months it's acquired more prominence because the nation's diminished confidence in his leadership has emboldened conservatives to be more outspoken about Bush's alleged betrayals of their cause. From the very inception of his candidacy, however, the president has sold himself as a "different kind of Republican," one who's willing to use government for affirmative purposes, one who cares about the poor. He and the larger Republican Party have sought to propagate a public image in which they desire just as much as any Democrat to adopt policies designed to broaden access to health insurance and to "strengthen Social Security."

Needless to say, this image is almost entirely a lie. Indeed, urging readers to pay less attention to what Bush *does* and more to what he *says* does not come naturally. The default instinct of a liberal journalist for the past several years has been to do the reverse. I and other bloggers have been documenting Bush's dissimulations on a daily basis, and the sheer scale of his dishonesty has inspired a cottage industry of books on the topic.

In the short term, such efforts to unmask the dark reality behind contemporary conservatism's happy self-portrait are vital. Only by succeeding in the task can we create the political circumstances in which progressive change will be possible. For the long term, however, the very fact of the lies is significant. The point is not so much that today's Republican leadership says things that aren't true—all politicians have done that since the dawn of time—but that they seek to fundamentally misrepresent their basic goals and approach to policy. This has worked as a political tactic, but it's a tactic born of underlying weakness. Gone is the bold rhetoric of the Reagan years when the right could forthrightly promise to get government off our backs and sweep to landslide reelection. Instead, Bush has eeked out narrow wins only by becoming what my colleague Bob Kuttner has called an "ideological impostor," a right-winger in liberal clothing.

Between Reaganism and Bushism there was, of course, the typically Clintonian dictum that "the era of big government is over, but we cannot go back to the time when our citizens were left to fend for themselves." What, exactly, this was supposed to mean was always hard to say. But Clinton's basic political project—the effort to rehabilitate faith in activist government by temporarily trimming its sails—has been strikingly successful, though he's tended not to get credit for it. His detractors on the left simply aren't in the habit of giving him credit for anything, while his fans have largely neglected the point because his very success has undermined much of the rationale for his approach.

Nevertheless, fewer than four years after he said those famous words, a sea change in American political culture was evident. Not only had the public become willing to accept a candidate who promised to preserve and extend the key elements of the welfare and regulatory states, they *demanded* candidates who would do so, to the point at which Republicans started pretending that they wanted this as well. When the Pew Research Center for People and the Press released its latest "political typology" in May 2005, they found the public could be divided into six basic types. Two of the three Republican voter blocks, along with all three of the Democratic ones, were found to be basically sympathetic to the cause of big government.

This is a tremendous opportunity. While Clinton, like Jimmy Carter before him, had to operate in a climate that was basically hostile to the liberal project, the next Democratic leader will operate under no such handicap. Instead, eight years of faux-liberalism and a conservative movement that has grown dependent on deception to maintain power will have paved the way for the real thing. For the first time since the mid-1960s, America is ready for political leadership that openly wants to use the power of government to do good and someday soon we may get a leader who actually means it.

Just don't let him call himself a liberal.